A
MONTH
of
FUNDAYS

A Whole Year of
Games and Activities for Just About
Every Holiday
You've Ever Heard of —
And Many That You Haven't!

Dawn DiPrince
and
Bonnie Benham, Susan Malmstadt
Amy Rider, Cheryl Miller Thurston

Cottonwood Press, Inc.
Fort Collins, Colorado

Requests for permission should be addressed to:

Cottonwood Press, Inc.
305 West Magnolia, Suite 398
Fort Collins, Colorado 80521

ISBN 1-877673-29-3

Cover by Patricia Howard

Printed in the United States of America

The activities in *A Month of Fundays* are organized by month, but who's to say you can't celebrate "Science Fiction Is So Fantastic Day" in October instead of February? If you want to use a November activity in March, feel free to do so. Joke with your students about mixing things up, or find another excuse for celebrating a holiday at the wrong time of year. The activities in *A Month of Fundays* are challenging and fun-to-do, no matter when you use them. We hope both you and your students will enjoy them.

The authors

Table of Contents

January

Unfit for human consumption?

National Oatmeal Month is sponsored by — what a surprise! — Quaker Oats Company, which hopes to encourage people to eat more oatmeal.

Many people, of course, eat oatmeal because they like it. Others eat it because they have heard about all its health benefits. Still others eat it because it's so easy to take a package of instant oatmeal and make a quick, hot breakfast.

But some people NEVER eat oatmeal. They absolutely hate the food and wouldn't eat it even if someone offered to pay them to take a bite.

Some foods are like that. They generate a lot of hate.

What food do you hate?

What food do you hate? Are tomatoes so disgusting that you can't let them touch any food on your plate? Does the thought of onion on a hamburger cause you to break out in a sweat? Are you afraid to even taste shredded wheat? Do poached eggs make you feel queasy, just looking at them?

Describe what is, in your opinion, the worst food in the world. Use words to let out all the negative feelings you have about this food.

Getting started

Start by listing adjectives that describe the food you hate. (Examples: *slimy, smelly, runny.*) Then list what the taste of this food does to you. (Examples: *gag, retch, recoil, double over, leave the room.*) Then list any other bad qualities the food has. (Examples: *It has an ugly color. It looks too much like dog food. It makes me break out in hives.*) Can you share any stories that involve your food? (Examples: *Once I ate some just before I got on Mr. Twister, the roller coaster. The results were just what you might expect.*) What else can you say about your food?

Now begin your rough draft. Tell why this food is unworthy of shelf space and should be banned from human consumption. (You might even want to share your paragraph with the person who cooks at your house!)

Answer key
Unfit for human consumption?

Answers will vary. Here is one possibility:

Tomatoes are by far the most disgusting, gross, revolting food on our planet. One of the worst things about them is that they get all over everything they touch. You put them in a salad, and they contaminate the dressing with their gloppy gunk and seeds. You put them on a sandwich or a hamburger, and they soggy up the bun with their juice. You try to scrape them off, and you can't. They have permanently destroyed your bread.

Whenever I help my mom cook dinner, she makes me slice the tomatoes. It is sheer torture. She says she gives me that job because she knows I won't nibble while I'm cooking. She is right. I get a sick feeling in the pit of my stomach just thinking about the juicy puddle of muck that is left on the cutting board.

The worst thing about tomatoes is that they are everywhere. At restaurants they can be found on salads, in sandwiches, on hamburgers, in tacos, on pizza and even as garnish. Wherever you look, there they are. I think tomatoes have become a bad American habit that should be stopped!

Gabriela N.

Love makes the world go 'round

In honor of Business and Reference Books Month, focus on four of the most useful reference books around: the thesaurus, the atlas, the dictionary and the almanac. Use these four reference books to complete the story "Andrew's Adventures with Love and Travel," below.

Andrew's Adventures with Love and Travel

"I love you," said Andrew, looking at Clarissa, the brilliant young scientist he wanted to marry.

"How ordinary," said Clarissa. "I'm attracted to men with large vocabularies. Can't you tell me you love me in more original words than that?"

Andrew sighed. "I'll be back in half an hour," he said.

He came back with a list. Here are the ten ways he told Clarissa that he loved her:

1. _____
2. _____
3. _____
4. _____
5. _____

6. _____
7. _____
8. _____
9. _____
10. _____

"Well, that's nice," said Clarissa, "but I'm afraid I don't love you at all. I never did, and I never will. In fact, I don't even like you very much."

Andrew stared at her. His love evaporated in an instant, and he stormed out of the room.

Half an hour later, he was back. "Hate is a very ordinary word," he said. "So instead of telling you that I now hate you, I will tell you the same thing in ten different ways. Take your pick:"

1. _____
2. _____
3. _____
4. _____
5. _____

6. _____
7. _____
8. _____
9. _____
10. _____

Andrew decided to forget about Clarissa by taking a trip around the world. First he visited the highest waterfall in the world: (1) _____ .

Then he traveled all the way across the second largest continent in the world, according to its area: (2) _____ .

Then he climbed the third highest mountain in the world: (3) _____ .

He visited a canal that connects the Pacific and Atlantic Oceans and is located in Central America. That canal is the (4) _____ .

He bought a car in Kansas City, Missouri, and decided to drive along Interstate 70 to Glenwood Springs, Colorado, to visit an old friend. The trip was about (5) _____ . miles.

Finally, Andrew was feeling a lot better. He came back home and decided to start a career. The problem was, he wasn't sure what that career should be. He thought about buying a *hartebeest,* a *wombat* and a *peccary* and starting a small (6) _____ .

He thought about learning to be a *prestidigitator* and doing (7) _____ .

He thought about buying an *escritoire,* a *chiffonier* and an *armoire* as the first items for a (8) _____ store.

He thought about buying a *xebec* and taking people on (9) _____ trips.

Finally, he decided what he really enjoyed was making things like *rouxs* and *junkets* and *kebabs.* "I'll be a (10) _____ !" he exclaimed.

His parents sent him to an excellent school, and he learned fast. Soon he was a great success. He had many friends, a wonderful home, a great car and a lovely and brilliant girlfriend named Melissa. He had been dating Melissa for eight months before he found enough courage to look into her eyes and say, "I love you, Melissa!"

"What beautiful words!" said Melissa.

Andrew knew that he would never think of Clarissa again. He was truly over her, forever.

Answer key
Love makes the world go 'round

Answers will vary. Here are a few possibilities:

Ten ways Andrew told Clarissa that he loved her:

1. I feel extreme affection for you.
2. You are my beloved.
3. I cherish you.
4. I am completely enamored with you.
5. I am completely captivated by you.
6. You have my very fond admiration and esteem.
7. I delight in your presence and hold you dear.
8. I am crazy about you.
9. I treasure everything about you.
10. I hold you in highest esteem, and then some.

Ten ways Andrew told Clarissa that he hated her:

1. I loathe you.
2. I feel enormous dislike for you.
3. Your presence disgusts me.
4. I detest your being.
5. I feel extreme revulsion toward you.
6. I despise you.
7. I find you abominable.
8. When I see you, I feel great hostility.
9. Your existence is repugnant to me.
10. You have no redeeming features at all.

1. Angel (in Venezuela)
2. Africa
3. Mount Kanchenjunga
4. Panama Canal
5. about 770 miles
6. zoo
7. magic
8. furniture
9. sailing trips
10. chef

Don't be cruel to blue suede shoes

January 8th is the birthday of one of America's most famous rock and roll singers — Elvis Presley. He may be dead, but his songs live on.

Actually, if you believe a few of his most enthusiastic fans, he isn't dead at all. Every year there are dozens of supposed "Elvis sightings," and some people insist that the man is really living in disguise somewhere in America.

Suppose for a moment that Elvis *is* living in disguise. Perhaps his songs should be disguised, too. Below is a list of some of his most famous songs. Using a dictionary, a thesaurus and your own brain, rewrite each title so that it is disguised. Use synonyms to create new titles that won't be so easily recognized. (Be sure you keep the meaning of each title the same, though.) This challenge is more fun if you have Elvis Presley music playing while you work!

Example

Love Me Tender:
Cherish Me Gently

1. Blue Suede Shoes _____

2. Stuck on You _____

3. A Big Hunk O' Love _____

4. All Shook Up _____

5. Are You Lonesome Tonight? _____

6. Can't Help Falling in Love _____

7. Jailhouse Rock _____

8. Viva Las Vegas _____

9. Return to Sender _____

10. (Ain't Nothin' But a) Hound Dog _____

11. Heartbreak Hotel _____

12. Teddy Bear _____

13. It's Now or Never _____

14. Crying in the Chapel _____

15. Don't Be Cruel _____

Bonus

Find out the words to an entire Elvis Presley song. Rewrite the words of the song in disguise. Again, keep the meaning the same as the original.

Answer key
Don't be cruel to blue suede shoes

Answers will vary. Here are a few possibilities:

1. Cobalt-Colored Leather Loafers
2. Attached with Glue to Another Person
3. An Enormous Piece of Strong Affection
4. Completely Agitated
5. Might You Be in Need of Some Company This Evening?
6. My Infatuation Is Unavoidable
7. Prison Dance
8. A Salute to a City in the Desert
9. Send It Back
10. Nothing Except for a Mutt
11. Unbearable Sadness Inn
12. Little Furry Stuffed Animal Named After a President
13. Either the Present or Not at All
14. Shedding Tears in a Small Place of Worship
15. Please Refrain from Being Sadistic

Bonus

Answers will vary. Here is one possibility:

Completely Agitated (All Shook Up)

Oh my, sanctify my essential spirit.
Is something amiss with my inner self?
I find myself with an irritating skin disease
like a guy on an unclear woody plant.
Those who know me and like me proclaim
that my behavior is as peculiar as an insect.
I'm enamored with someone!
I'm completely agitated!

Vibrations occur on the appendages of my front limbs,
and the middle joints of my legs are without strength.
I cannot stay upright on the two body parts
contained in my shoes.
I question where I should direct my appreciation
in the event of such good fortune.
I'm enamored with someone!
I'm completely agitated! (etc.)

What's the good word?

Have you ever been brain-tied? Brain-tied is a bit like tongue-tied, except that it is your brain instead of your voice that won't work correctly. When you're brain-tied, you KNOW that there is a word for something you want to express, but you just can't get your brain to bring that word into focus.

That's where a thesaurus comes in handy. A thesaurus lists synonyms for hundreds and hundreds of words. You can look up a word that is close to the meaning you want, and chances are you will find just the word you want — or maybe even a better one.

January 18th is Thesaurus Day, a day dedicated to appreciating the thesaurus. In honor of this day, complete the challenging exercise below.

Baby, airplane, math teacher and telephone make news

1. The title above is the headline for an imaginary newspaper story. What happened? What is the story about? That's for *you* to decide. See if you can come up with an idea for a newspaper story that would fit the headline.

2. Now try writing your newspaper story — but with one catch. You must use at least ten of the words in the list below. (Note: It's okay to use a different form of a word, like "departed" instead of "depart.")

red	choice	flashy
cup	passenger	growl
eat	big	escape
toy	sound	pursue
activity	silence	travel
depart	thief	ugly
ledge	many	

3. Now go back and replace the ten ordinary words with interesting synonyms. (In case you have forgotten, synonyms are words that share the same meaning, or approximately the same meaning.) Use a thesaurus, of course, for help.

4. Write a new headline for your story. Be sure to include an active verb. An active verb is one that has someone *doing* something. (Examples: Baby *hijacks* airplane. Math teacher *invents* combination telephone/coffee maker.)

Answer key
What's the good word?

Answers will vary. Here is one example:

Math teacher and baby capture "Telephone Bomber" and save airplane

Ellen Eagleton, a math teacher from Portland, Oregon, and her nine-month-old baby, Emma, have succeeded where the FBI and other law enforcement agencies failed. Yesterday they snared the Telephone Bomber. They also saved an airplane full of commuters (**passengers**) from the Telephone Bomber's latest bomb.

Eagleton and her baby were seated next to the bomber, Maxwell Malice, on an airplane destined for Tallahassee, Florida. Eagleton was wary of the man next to her: "When he sat down, he made a hideous (**ugly**) face at Emma and then grumbled (**growled**) at me."

After everyone finished dining (**eating**) and the flight attendants picked up the lunch mess, Malice pulled out an old black rotary telephone from his duffel bag under the seat in front of him. Malice reached inside the hollow phone and withdrew a homemade explosive device wrapped in a scarlet (**red**) handkerchief. When Emma caught a glimpse of the scarlet handkerchief, she tried to reach for it. Her favorite plaything (**toy**) is a kitty cat made with the same material as the handkerchief.

When Eagleton looked to see what her daughter was crying about, she noticed the telephone. When Malice detected the suspicious look on Eagleton's face, he jumped to his feet and tried to flee (**escape**). Eagleton quickly handed her baby to the teen-age girl across the aisle and then tackled Malice. The flight attendants put Malice in custody until the plane landed.

Malice allegedly injured 134 people in 45 different bombing attacks. The FBI has been chasing (**pursuing**) the Telephone Bomber for the last 16 years. He is called the Telephone Bomber because an old black rotary telephone is found at the scene of every attack.

The Telephone Bomber's victims have all been tourists, and most attacks have been in the summer when numerous (**many**) people are globetrotting (**traveling**). His intent seems to have been *not* to kill — no deaths have resulted from his attacks — but to stop people from traveling. Police speculate that he hates tourists.

When asked how she felt about being lauded a hero, Eagleton said, "Emma is the real hero!"

Alicia S.

Quoth the raven nevermore

January 19 is the birthday of Edgar Allan Poe, the famous writer. He is known as the creator of the short story. He is also famous for his tales of horror. You may have read or listened to some of his works, like "The Tell-Tale Heart" or "The Pit and the Pendulum."

One of Poe's most famous works is the poem "The Raven," with the famous line, "Quoth the raven, 'Nevermore.'" As you read aloud or listen to "The Raven," notice how much rhyming there is in the poem, both at the end of lines and in the middle of lines. Also notice how many words rhyme with "or."

Now, in honor of Poe's birthday, see how many "or" rhymes you can come up with. For each definition below, fill in a word that rhymes with "or."

1. What most children want, after just a taste of ice cream _____

2. Horror movies often have a lot of this _____

3. Sometimes bickering brothers and sisters seem to want to start one _____

4. An apple's insides _____

5. What you take if you give a speech in front of a group _____

6. Someone who talks endlessly of his aches and pains and pills might be described as one

    _____

7. A morning hour when most people don't want to hear an alarm _____

8. What you hope not to be surprised by, if walking in the jungle _____

9. Where trick or treaters gather _____

10. What a boring teacher tempts you to do _____

11. Where you can buy your favorite mystery _____

12. A branch of the U.S. Armed Forces is the Marine _____

Now add three more definitions of your own to this puzzle. Remember: The answers must rhyme with "or." Be sure to include an answer key.

1. _____

2. _____

3. _____

Bonus

Write a short poem of your own. In honor of Edgar Allan Poe's birthday, use a number of "or" rhymes, and make the subject of the poem something "raven-ish" — perhaps something frightening or creepy.

Answer key
Quoth the raven nevermore

1. more
2. gore
3. war
4. core
5. the floor
6. bore
7. four
8. roar (or a boar)
9. door
10. snore
11. bookstore
12. Corps

Answers will vary for the following. Here are three possibilities:

1. What you do when your dad is giving you a lecture (ignore).
2. Loading the dishwasher is something you (abhor).
3. Ghost stories are (folklore).

Bonus

Answers will vary. Here is one possibility:

I opened the door
and heard a roar
and saw the gore
there on the floor.
And then a four-toed,
bug-eyed Blore
devoured my fish
and wanted more.
He ate the couch
and our back door.
He wasn't something
to ignore.
I think I hate that
bug-eyed Blore!

John Z.

Pop! Pop! Pop! Pop! Pop! Pop!

National Popcorn Day — January 29

National Popcorn Day honors, of course, popcorn. Think about all the uses for popcorn — something to munch on at the movies, something to string for Christmas tree decorations, an easy snack to make in the microwave.

Celebrate National Popcorn Day by opening up your mind and coming up with 25 *new* uses for popcorn — *other* than eating it. Think about how it looks on the cob, in a jar, popped in a pan. Open your mind to creative possibilities.

1. _____
2. _____
3. _____
4. _____
5. _____
6. _____
7. _____
8. _____
9. _____
10. _____
11. _____
12. _____
13. _____
14. _____
15. _____
16. _____
17. _____
18. _____
19. _____
20. _____
21. _____
22. _____
23. _____
24. _____
25. _____

Bonus

Create a picture or an actual model of one of your new uses for popcorn.

Answer key
Pop! Pop! Pop! Pop! Pop! Pop!

Answers will vary. Here are some possibilities:

1. (unpopped) Use it to fill bean bags.
2. (on the cob) Use it for fall table centerpieces.
3. (popped) Stick pieces into Styrofoam to make a wreath.
4. (popped) Use it as packaging material for fragile objects.
5. (popped) Use it for fake snow if you live where there is no snow.
6. (unpopped) Superglue it all over an empty can to make a pencil holder.
7. (popped) Stuff it in a mattress for soft bedding.
8. (popped) Put it on a string to make a dress-up necklace for little kids.
9. (popped) Make many strings and hang in a doorway to take the place of a beaded cur-tain.
10. (unpopped) Put it in jars and shake, to make a musical instrument.
11. (unpopped) Stuff socks with it to make weights for working out.
12. (unpopped) Stuff a sock with it and use it for a doorstop.
13. (unpopped) Use it to replace the stuffing in an old beanbag chair.
14. (unpopped) Put it in a jar and use it as a paperweight.
15. (popped) Put glue on a ceiling and attach popcorn, instead of texturing the ceiling.
16. (popped) Put a wire through a piece and use it as an earring you can eat after wearing.
17. (popped) Use it for insulation in the winter.
18. (popped) Use it instead of gauze after dental work.
19. (popped) Feed the birds with it.
20. (popped) Use it to play catch with your dog.
21. (popped) Use it as a lure on a mouse trap, especially if it's cheese-flavored.
22. (unpopped) Use it instead of gravel in the driveway.
23. (popped) Use it in potting soil instead of Styrofoam balls to aerate the soil.
24. (unpopped) Use it instead of colored rock to landscape your yard.
25. (unpopped) Use it in a vase to hold dried flower arrangements.

Bonus

Answers will vary. Here is one possibility:

I have a dream

Dr. Martin Luther King believed in nonviolence as a way to promote change. During the 1960s, he traveled in the South, preaching his message of peaceful demonstrations and civil rights for blacks.

In August, 1963, Dr. King gave a speech that has gone down in history. He spoke to approximately 200,000 people who were marching in Washington, D.C. They were demonstrating their support for civil rights. Here is part of what he said in this famous speech:

> *I have a dream that one day this nation will rise up, live out the true meaning of its creed: "We hold these truths to be self-evident, that all men are created equal." I have a dream that one day on the red hills of Georgia sons of former slaves and the sons of former slave-owners will be able to sit down together at the table of brotherhood. I have a dream that one day even the state of Mississippi, a state sweltering with the heat of injustice . . . will be transformed into an oasis of freedom and justice. I have a dream that my four little children will one day live in a nation where they will not be judged by the color of their skin but by the content of their character.*

Take a look at Dr. King's words. What he said is important, of course. However, the *way* he said it helped make his words effective. Imagine if he had summed up his thoughts something like this:

> *Someday I hope people in this country will really be equal. Then people everywhere will be able to associate with one another. The state of Mississippi has been an unjust state in the past, but maybe someday it will be over all that. Someday I hope that no one will care about the color of a person's skin. People will look at what is really important: a person's character.*

Even though the meaning is the same, this version of the speech lacks the impact of the first version. It is doubtful that anyone would ever remember these words. Go back to Dr. King's original speech. Notice four things he did to make his words memorable:

- He repeated the words "I have a dream." This repetition is almost musical, like the repetition of a chorus in a song.

- He created an image we can see: sons of former slaves and slave-owners sitting down together. Notice that he doesn't have them sitting down at any old table. He has them doing something greater: sitting at the table of brotherhood.

- He created an image of perfection: Mississippi doesn't just get better. It becomes an *oasis* of freedom and justice.

- Finally, he created a personal image: his own "four little children" living in a country where they are judged by their character, not the color of their skin.

Creating your own "I have a dream" speech

Try following Dr. King's example. In honor of Martin Luther King's birthday (celebrated the third Monday in January), create your own "I have a dream" speech for the world or for America. Choose a serious subject for this speech, not a dream about getting rid of television commercials or making Homer Simpson a candidate for president. Choose a subject that would affect the country or the world in a serious and positive way. For example, you might talk about solutions to the problems of hunger, homelessness, war, divorce, etc.

Make your speech about as long as the excerpt from Dr. King's speech. Like Dr. King, repeat the words "I have a dream." Also, follow his example and create three images in your speech: an image we can see, an image of perfection and a personal image.

Answer key
I have a dream

Answers will vary. Here is one possibility:

War

I have a dream that one day human beings everywhere will put down their hatchets, assault guns and nuclear weapons and finally fulfill the often-spoken words, "Let there be peace on earth." I have a dream that one day on playgrounds, in day care centers, at recess and after school, children all over the world will no longer play with guns or mimic war, and they will understand that war is a thing of the past. I have a dream that one day I may set foot on the streets of my great grandmother's birthplace in Serbia and hear — not the deadly silence interrupted only by mortar rounds — but the alive sounds of children playing in a bustling city.

Marielena A.

Good fortune will be yours

Most people enjoy opening a fortune cookie and reading the message inside. Sometimes, however, the message is pretty boring. Who can get excited about a message like "The future is yours to grab" or "Hard work is its own reward"?

In honor of Chinese New Year (sunset on the day of the second new moon after the winter solstice), try your hand at writing fortunes — *interesting* fortunes. The fortunes should all be one sentence in length. As for subject matter, you may try one or both of the following approaches:

- Write fortunes that apply to people of all ages. In other words, don't write a fortune that would make sense only for a ten-year-old boy. Make the message more general. (Examples: *You will never again have a bad hair day . . . Lots of money is coming your way.*)

- Write special fortune cookies that apply only to young people. Assume that no adults will receive these special fortune cookies. (Examples: *The girl or boy of your dreams will soon ask you for a date . . . You will never again have math homework.*)

Your fortunes can include predictions about the future, bits of advice, observations about life — whatever you think would be interesting. Remember that restaurants give fortune cookies to their customers, so they don't want to offend or annoy them. Who would want to keep coming back to a restaurant with fortunes like, "You are going to be hit by a truck and suffer terribly" or "No one on the face of the earth is as ugly as you"? Keep your messages optimistic and kind.

1. _____
2. _____
3. _____
4. _____
5. _____
6. _____
7. _____
8. _____
9. _____
10. _____
11. _____
12. _____

Bonus

Find a recipe for fortune cookies. Just for the fun of it, try making your own cookies and putting your interesting fortunes inside.

Answer key
Good fortune will be yours

Answers will vary. Here are some possibilities:

1. Scientists will soon discover the nutritious benefits of junk food.
2. Pimples will never be a problem for you.
3. Ed McMahon will soon be ringing your door bell.
4. You are smarter than anyone who has ever appeared on the television show "Jeopardy."
5. You would be very surprised if you knew who thinks you are great looking.
6. "Coolness" comes from the inside.
7. Remember the hardships of being a teenager so that you will be a more understanding adult.
8. Five minutes of fun is not worth two weeks of being grounded.
9. The person you marry will love pizza with black olives and pineapple.
10. A clean locker is its own reward.
11. In algebra lies the meaning of life.
12. Be careful of the notes you pass; they may be intercepted.

February

Ten times ten

Since 1926, Black History Month has acknowledged the achievements of Afro-Americans. Celebrate the contributions of black men and women from America as well as the rest of the world by creating a "tens poster." A tens poster is a poster that highlights ten different people, giving ten pieces of information about each of them. The poster can include drawings, pictures, symbols, magazine cutouts or diagrams to make it interesting and attractive.

On your tens poster, be sure to include each individual's name and the years that the person lived. Below that, list the ten facts or items of interest.

Example

Martin Luther King, Jr. (1929 to 1968)

1. He led the civil rights movement in America.
2. He believed in nonviolence as the most effective approach to creating change.
3. He was assassinated in 1968 by James Earl Ray.
4. He was a minister in a Montgomery, Alabama, church.
5. He received the Kennedy Peace Prize in 1964.
6. He received the Nobel Peace Prize in 1964.
7. He organized the boycott of city buses in Montgomery, Alabama.
8. He led the first march for civil rights on Washington, D.C.
9. He gave his famous "I Have a Dream" speech in Washington, D.C.
10. He was inspired by Henry David Thoreau and Mahatma Gandhi.

Below is a list of 100 of the countless black men and women who have contributed to history. Some are making history right now, while others contributed many years ago. This selection of names represents people from a wide variety of fields, from science and politics to arts and entertainment. Choose people from this list for your poster, or feel free to choose other notable black men and women who are not listed here.

1. Henry Louis (Hank) Aaron — baseball player who broke Babe Ruth's career home run record

2. Ralph D. Abernathy — leader of the civil rights movement and one of the founders of the Southern Christian Leadership Conference

3. Muhammad Ali — first man to win the world heavyweight title three times

4. Marian Anderson — classical singer and goodwill ambassador for the United States

5. Maya Angelou — poet, author and actor who read her poem "Still I Rise" at Bill Clinton's presidential inauguration

6. Louis Armstrong — musician who had a great influence on trumpet style and helped gain recognition for jazz throughout the world

7. Arthur Ashe — first African-American male to win the U.S. Open

8. Crispus Attucks — escaped slave killed at the Boston Massacre while protesting the presence of British soldiers in the Colonies

9. Josephine Baker — entertainer and civil rights activist awarded the Legion of Honor for helping the Resistance in World War II

10. James Baldwin — civil rights activist and author of several novels, including the well-known *Go Tell It On the Mountain*

11. Mary McLeod Bethune — pioneer of African-American education and the president of the National Council of Negro Women

12. Guion S. Bluford, Jr. — NASA astronaut and first African-American to fly in space

13. Ed Bradley — television journalist and co-editor of "60 Minutes"

14. Gwendolyn Brooks — Pulitzer Prize-winning poet and author

15. Ron Brown — Secretary of Commerce in the Clinton administration and first African-American to chair a major political party

16. Ralph J. Bunche — United Nations mediator who arranged for a cease-fire in Palestine and was awarded the Nobel Peace Prize

17. Thomas Cab Calloway — bandleader, singer and composer known as the "Hi-De-Ho Man"

18. Stokely Carmichael — civil rights leader who was spokesman for the black power movement

19. Diahann Carroll — the first black star of a situation comedy, "Julia"

20. George Washington Carver — teacher and scientist who researched agricultural problems and developed peanut butter

21. Elizabeth Catlett — world-renowned sculptor and painter

22. Ray Charles — singer and pianist whose new style of rhythm and blues proved widely influential in the music world

23. Shirley Chisholm — first black woman in Congress

24. Johnnetta Cole — scholar and anthropologist who also became the first black woman president of Spelman College

25. Nat "King" Cole — popular singer known for his rendition of the song "Mona Lisa"

26. Bill Cosby — popular Emmy-award winning actor and comedian

27. Miles Davis — trumpeter and composer who introduced the style known as "cool jazz"

28. Sammy Davis, Jr. — singer, dancer, comedian and actor known for his tremendous versatility

29. Frederick Douglass — eloquent abolitionist who struggled for over fifty years against slavery

30. Charles R. Drew — surgeon and blood plasma expert whose work led to storage of plasma in blood banks

31. Katherine Dunham — dancer, choreographer and anthropologist who promoted Caribbean black culture

Copyright © 1996 Cottonwood Press, Inc. • 305 West Magnolia, Suite 398 • Fort Collins, Colorado 80521

32. W.E.B. DuBois — co-founder of the NAACP and the first African-American to hold a doctorate from Harvard

33. Marian Wright Edelman — spokesperson for needy children and their families and founder of the Children's Defense Fund

34. Duke Ellington — big band leader and one of the most influential African-American composers of the twentieth century

35. Louis Farrakhan — leader of the Nation of Islam and organizer of the Million Man March

36. Ella Fitzgerald — singer known around the world as the "First Lady of Song"

37. Aretha Franklin — singer and winner of ten Grammy Awards

38. Marcus Garvey — controversial promoter of a return of blacks to the "African Motherland"

39. Althea Gibson — first black tennis player to compete at Wimbledon

40. Savion Glover — tap dancer and choreographer known for his hit show *Bring in 'da Noise, Bring in 'da Funk*

41. Earl Graves — founder of the monthly magazine *Black Enterprise*, which annually lists and ranks the top 100 black businesses in America

42. Bill Gray — theologian and Congressman who became the first black to chair the powerful House Budget Committee

43. Dick Gregory — comedian and civil and human rights activist

44. Bryant Gumble — journalist and host of the "Today Show"

45. Alex Haley — author whose books, including *Roots* and *Queenie*, stimulated new interest in black genealogy

46. Lorraine Hansberry — first black playwright to have a show on Broadway

47. James Healy — first African-American to be ordained a Roman Catholic priest

48. Patrick Healy — first African-American president of a predominantly white university (Georgetown University)

49. Anita Hill — professor of law who helped raise awareness of sexual harassment

50. Billie Holiday — ballad singer whose autobiography, *Lady Sings the Blues*, told of her troubled life

51. Lena Horne — singer and actress whose most popular recordings include "Stormy Weather" and "Mad About the Boy"

52. Langston Hughes — poet, novelist, and playwright well-known for his poems "Dream Boogie" and "A Dream Deferred"

53. Zora Neale Hurston — influential writer whose first work was published in 1921

54. Jesse Jackson — Baptist minister and politician who advised Dr. King and sought the U.S. presidency in 1984 and 1988

55. Mahalia Jackson — gospel and blues artist who sang at President Kennedy's inauguration

56. Michael Jackson — singer known around the world as the "King of Pop Music"

57. John H. Johnson — publisher of *Ebony* magazine and listed by *Forbes* magazine as one of the four hundred richest people in America

58. James Earl Jones — actor whose deep and resonating voice was the voice of Darth Vader in the *Star Wars* trilogy

59. Scott Joplin — ragtime music composer known as the "King of Ragtime"

60. Michael Jordan — basketball player whose great skill and popularity have brought him fame and fortune

61. Barbara Jordan — member of the U.S. Congress who gave the keynote speech at the 1976 Democratic National Convention

62. Florence Griffith Joyner — Olympic champion sprinter who was dubbed "the fastest woman in the world" at the 1988 Olympics

63. Jackie Joyner-Kersee — Olympic champion runner and triple-jumper

64. Spike Lee — film director whose movies include *Do the Right Thing, Mo' Better Blues* and *Crooklyn*

65. Joe Louis — world heavyweight boxing champion from 1937 to 1949

66. Malcolm X — leader of the Nation of Islam who later founded his own movement and was assassinated in 1965

67. Nelson Mandela — civil rights activist who became the first black leader of South Africa

68. Thurgood Marshall — first African-American Supreme Court Justice

69. James Meredith — college student whose enrollment in the all-white University of Mississippi caused campus rioting and the call-up of 13,000 federal troops

70. Oscar Micheaux — filmmaker who eventually formed his own film company to change the "negative images blacks have had of themselves" through white-produced and directed films

71. Toni Morrison — author of many novels including *Jazz, Song of Solomon* and *Beloved,* which earned her the Pulitzer Prize for fiction in 1988

72. Jelly Roll Morton — pioneer in jazz composition and leader of the band Red Hot Peppers

73. Jesse Owens — athlete who was shunned by Hitler at the 1936 Olympics but won four gold medals and set five world records in track

74. Charlie "Bird" Parker — jazz musician who helped develop the style known as "bebop"

75. Rosa Parks — seamstress whose refusal to give up her seat on a city bus ignited the civil rights movement in the United States

76. Sidney Poitier — first black actor to win an Oscar for a leading role

77. Colin Powell — military general who led operations in Desert Storm

78. Jackie Robinson — first African-American professional baseball player

79. Carl Rowan — prominent journalist and former director of the United States Information Agency

80. Wilma Rudolph — Olympic athlete of track and field

81. Edith Spurlock Sampson — first African-American woman judge

82. Ntozake Shange — poet, novelist and playwright who wrote *For Colored Girls Who Have Considered Suicide/ When the Rainbow Is Enuf*

83. Arthur Schomburg — "the Sherlock Holmes of Negro History" who collected documents, books and artifacts relating to black history

84. John Singletary — director whose movies include *Boyz N the Hood* (at age 23) and *Poetic Justice*

85. Art Shell — first African-American head coach in the NFL

86. Bessie Smith — singer known as the "Empress of Blues"

87. Clarence Thomas — Supreme Court Justice whose nomination hearing brought forward the issue of sexual harassment in the work place

88. Sojourner Truth — abolitionist and women's rights activist known for her "Ain't I a Woman" speech

89. Harriet Tubman — abolitionist who used the Underground Railroad to help lead over 300 slaves to freedom

90. Nat Turner — leader of an 1831 Virginia slave revolt

91. Archbishop Desmond Tutu — South African religious leader who was an important force in ending apartheid

92. Madame C.J. Walker — first known African-American female millionaire, who made her fortune by developing beauty care prodcuts for blacks

93. Alice Walker — Pulitzer Prize-winning author of *The Color Purple* and other books

94. Booker T. Washington — speaker, writer and educator who made Tuskegee Institute a major establishment for African-American education

95. Denzel Washington — actor known for his role in the movies *Philadelphia, Mo' Better Blues, Glory,* and *Malcolm X*

96. Phillis Wheatley — poet whose work was used by abolitionists to disprove charges of intellectual inferiority among African-Americans

97. August Wilson — American playwright whose works include *Ma Rainey's Black Bottom* and *Two Trains Running*

98. Oprah Winfrey — actor, TV talk-show host and president of Harpo Studios, Inc.

99. Richard Wright — author of several novels, including *Native Son,* and an autobiography titled *Black Boy*

100. Andrew Jackson Young, Jr. — civil rights activist and Congressman who worked for human rights throughout the world

Mr. or Ms. Perfect?

No matter how much we like a president of the United States, Americans always manage to find flaws with him. Perhaps we don't like his stance on an important issue. Perhaps we think he is not a very good speaker. Perhaps we hate the way he dresses or the way he talks. As a group, we can be pretty picky.

See if you can come up with the ideal candidate for president — one who would be as close to perfect as possible, at least from your perspective. Imagine a candidate so perfect that he or she would escape criticism, at least from you.

In imagining this candidate, consider the following:

- What important issues does he or she stand for? What are his or her views?

- How is he or she like former presidents? How is he or she different?

- Why is this person so ideal for the presidency?

Describe your candidate. Then create *one* of the following for your candidate's campaign:

- a speech

- a brochure

- a radio commercial

- a television commercial

Answer key
Mr. or Ms. Perfect?

Answers will vary. Here is one example:

My ideal candidate would be a 15-year-old young woman with a vision for the future. Her vision would be to make the world a better place for children. Since she would still be a minor herself, she would be the best person for the job.

She would be like no other president before her for two reasons — her gender and her age. These two things would be a plus because she would bring a new perspective and new ideas to the White House.

A speech for the perfect president

"Children are our future," everyone says. But looking at the state of things recently, I believe that one of two things must be true. Either people don't truly believe this statement, or people don't really care about the future. Children today are growing up in a world that is unkind to them.

Fourteen million children under the age of six live in poverty. Studies have shown that with poverty comes an increased chance of malnutrition and criminal behavior. With poverty comes an overall decreased chance of success. That is not the right way to treat our future. Child abuse is still a very prevalent problem. That is not the right way to treat our future. School age children have to go to school in fear of the violence that may lurk there. That is not the right way to treat our future.

I'm here to tell you that I can ensure a brighter future. I am better able to do this because I'm "only" 15 years old, which means that I am part of the future. I'm going to be around a lot longer than the older candidates, so I have a genuine stake in the future of our world. Those of us under the age of 18 are the only citizens in this country who do not have the right to vote. Someone needs to be the voice of my generation, and I am that voice.

Unlike the presidents before me, I truly want what is right for children, and that means hope for a better future. A better future would mean an environment where the air is clean, the trees are green and humans and animals can live in harmony. A better future would mean safe schools that demand the best from children and give them the best. A better future would mean good health care available to children all over our nation. A better future would mean programs set up to help families get out of poverty. A better future would be a safe world where children can play together. If what you want is a better, brighter future, then vote for me.

Gabriela M.

Brave new world

Here's your chance to be in charge of the world. Actually, you get to do more than be in charge. You get to *create* a world.

Science fiction writers create new worlds all of the time. They also break rules. They don't have to follow the rules and laws of real life in their work, the way most writers do. For example, a science fiction writer might decide that the law of gravity doesn't apply in her story. Or she might create a universe where brains are located in the elbow. Or she might create a planet where people are born old and get younger over the years.

In honor of "Science Fiction Is So Fantastic Day," create the setting for a science fiction story. You don't actually have to write the story. Just imagine and describe the world where the story might take place.

Getting started

The setting for your world might be the present, the future or the past. It might be the earth, another planet, a space ship, another dimension, another universe or somewhere else entirely. Think about the kind of world you want to create.

Give the place a name. Then tell how it is different from the world as we know it. Who lives there? How are the inhabitants different from humans? How do they survive? What do they eat or drink? How do they breathe? What type of government rules this world? Stretch your mind.

Describe your setting in detail.

Bonus

Make a drawing of the world you imagine, to go along with your written description.

Answer key
Brave new world

Answers will vary. Here is one example:

In a galaxy far, far away, there is a planet named Emptoid. This planet is about the same size as the earth and from the outside doesn't look like much more than an oversized asteroid. However, at the very center of the somber shell is a *man-made sun*. This sun isn't like a light bulb. It is composed of a carefully mixed combination of gasses, much like the earth's sun. However, the inhabitants of this planet are able to control the amount of energy this sun emits.

Why is there a sun inside Emptoid? Emptoid was found by some lost colonists looking for a new home. They noticed that the planet was hollow and, using their advanced technology, created a paradise inside. This included making a sun at the very center of the planet. However, they didn't plan very well. They forgot about the special rules for living *inside* a planet. If the people who run the sun fall asleep on the job, the planet can get very, very hot. The inhabitants of Emptoid had to dig vents into outer space, so they could open the vents during emergencies. Something else they didn't plan on was not being able to shut off the sun to make night. Therefore, it is sunny and warm *all the time* inside Emptoid. This makes it very hard to keep track of time, so people end up working long, long hours and sleeping very little.

Because the sun is always on, the people inside get very tan. They also become wrinkled at a very early age, because of all the exposure to the sun. Even teenagers try every wrinkle cream product that is advertised, hoping that *this* one will really work.

Emptoid is also a wonderful place to grow food. Since the sun is always shining and the temperature is always the same (unless the sun people fall asleep, of course), every imaginable type of food grows very well. The people of Emptoid are never hungry, and, in fact, almost everyone is somewhat chubby. To keep from getting even chubbier, people run everywhere they go.

Thad H.

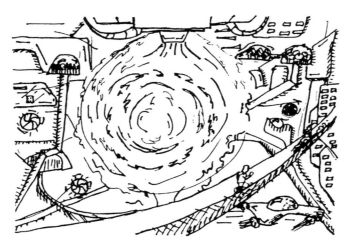

Emptoid

Eureka! I think I've got it!

Thomas Alva Edison is known as one of the world's greatest inventors. He invented many conveniences of the modern world, including the electric light bulb, the phonograph and motion picture equipment. However, Edison's inventions weren't always all that popular. He sometimes invented items that weren't really needed or weren't well-received, including an electric mousetrap and an electric vote recorder that made vote tabulation faster and more accurate.

In honor of National Inventor's Day, help inventors avoid Edison's problem. Give them a list of 25 things that need to be invented. What would make your life easier? Less stressful? More fun? Don't worry about whether or not your invention seems *possible*. After all, people told the Wright brothers it "couldn't be done," but they went ahead and flew the first heavier-than-air machine anyway. Inventors need a certain sense of playfulness. Instead of thinking about what might be *possible*, think about what would be *great*.

Examples

Automatic tooth flossers
Windshields that won't hold ice
Self-baiting fish hooks
Locker deodorizers

1. _____
2. _____
3. _____
4. _____
5. _____
6. _____
7. _____
8. _____
9. _____
10. _____
11. _____
12. _____
13. _____

14. _____
15. _____
16. _____
17. _____
18. _____
19. _____
20. _____
21. _____
22. _____
23. _____
24. _____
25. _____

Answer key
Eureka! I think I've got it!

Answers will vary. Here are some possibilities:

1. automatic bed maker
2. no-fat french fries that taste good
3. automatic chocolate chip cookie-making machine
4. pill for perfect hair
5. shoes that turn into boots when it snows
6. same-day seeds that grow flowers in 24 hours
7. baby quieter that activates when a baby awakens at night
8. remote control that cuts out commercials
9. pencil that makes all handwriting legible
10. self-emptying trash can
11. buzzer that goes off if you forget to take out your contacts
12. cat litter box that flushes
13. pimple preventer that really works
14. pill for straightening teeth overnight, eliminating the need for braces
15. remote control that won't permit rapid channel surfing, except if the operator is alone in the room
16. alarm clock that also makes you breakfast
17. grocery bags that float up to your third floor apartment so you don't have to carry them up yourself
18. books that automatically open to the last page you were reading
19. laundry that sorts itself
20. good-tasting stamp glue
21. smock that you could program to turn into any outfit you want
22. hat that won't give you "hat head"
23. another day of the week
24. diapers that don't smell
25. automatic clothes folding device that attaches to the dryer

Mushy stuff

Valentine's Day is considered the day of love and romance and, according to many young people, "all that mushy stuff."

As a Valentine's Day challenge, complete the Valentine's story started below. Your story may be as mushy or as non-mushy as you like, but the story must include at least four of the following: *hearts, flowers, candy, a valentine, cupid, a romantic gift* or *the words "I love you!"*

It was a dark and stormy night, but Emily didn't care. It didn't matter that lightning had just struck the elm tree out back, or that thunder was terrifying the dog, or that rain was leaking through the window. _____

_____

Answer key
Mushy stuff

Answers will vary. Here is one example:

It was a dark and stormy night, but Emily didn't care. It didn't matter that lightning had just struck the elm tree out back, or that thunder was terrifying the dog, or that rain was leaking through the window. This was her 16th birthday, and she wasn't going to let anything upset her. Having **a valentine** birthday wasn't always fun because people were so caught up in giving **flowers** or **candy**-filled **hearts** to each other that they didn't spend a lot of time getting her good presents. And she always got birthday cards with corny looking **cupids** from her grandparents and her aunts.

But this year was different. Emily had told everyone that she didn't want any reminder of **valentines** or **hearts** on her 16th birthday. She and her three best girlfriends had just eaten a birthday dinner of lasagna and salad, and now the girls were watching as Emily opened the presents they had brought her.

But Emily didn't know whether to laugh or cry as she unwrapped the gifts. Jody's present was a gold bracelet with a red **heart** dangling from it. Marissa gave her a stuffed bear holding a **heart** that said **"I love you!"** and Harriet had made her a huge **heart**-shaped pillow with a stupid looking **cupid** sewed on the top. Nobody had listened to her, even her best friends!

Just as she tried to smile and thank them, the three girls burst out laughing, rolling on the floor and slapping each other on the back. Emily wondered what was going on.

"Now would you like your real gifts?" Harriet asked. Just then Marissa brought in three more gifts wrapped in blue, purple and yellow — no red **hearts** or stupid **cupids** this time.

Emily laughed as she tore open the packages.

Nichole R.

Dripsteens' Yad

All of the scrambled words below are associated — rightly or wrongly — with the presidents honored on Presidents' Day (the third Monday in February): George Washington and Abraham Lincoln. Unscramble these anagrams. Then tell briefly how the item is associated with Lincoln or Washington.

Example

SHOTEN BEA:
Honest Abe (Lincoln's nickname)

1. HERRCY REET _____
2. VICLI RAW _____
3. ATHARM _____
4. RAYM DOTD _____
5. LEAVLY GORFE _____
6. DREEPDOW GWI _____
7. SANISTANOSIAS _____
8. DOWONE HETET _____
9. DRABE _____
10. HONJ SLEWKI THOBO _____
11. NEXTITHES _____
12. LARGEEN _____
13. IVARTULEYORNO RAW _____
14. UNTOM ROVENN _____
15. GLO BINCA _____
16. OIVEPPETS THA _____
17. DROF'S HATERET _____
18. OLDRAL LILB _____
19. GRUBSTYTEG SADSERD _____
20. WRADELAE VERIR _____

Bonus

Now add at least three items of your own to the puzzle above. Be sure to include an answer key.

Answer key
Dripsteens' Yad

1. cherry tree (what Washington supposedly cut down)
2. Civil War (occurred when Lincoln was president)
3. Martha (wife of Washington)
4. Mary Todd (wife of Lincoln)
5. Valley Forge (Washington's headquarters during the winter of 1777-78)
6. powdered wig (Washington wore one.)
7. assassination (how Lincoln died)
8. wooden teeth (what Washington supposedly wore for false teeth)
9. beard (Lincoln had one.)
10. John Wilkes Booth (killed Lincoln)
11. sixteenth (Lincoln was the 16th president.)
12. General (Washington's title)
13. Revolutionary War (Washington fought in this.)
14. Mount Vernon (where Washington lived)
15. log cabin (where Lincoln was born)
16. stovepipe hat (what Lincoln wore)
17. Ford's Theatre (where Lincoln was killed)
18. dollar bill (Washington is on it.)
19. Gettysburg Address (what Lincoln presented)
20. Delaware River (Washington crossed it.)

Bonus

Answers will vary. Here are some possibilities:

1. TRIFS DRIPSTEEN: first President (what Washington was)
2. ORFU REOCS DNA: Four score and (the beginning of the "Gettysburg Address")
3. STONCITNUTIO: Constitution (Washington urged its ratification)

Kindness is catching

In the early 1980s, a California writer named Anne Herbert came up with the phrase "Practice random kindness and senseless acts of beauty." Soon the phrase started appearing on bumper stickers all over the country, and today there are more and more people who support a "Kindness Movement." Supporters perform simple acts of kindness, usually anonymously. For example, they might shovel the neighbor's walk when doing their own, throw a newspaper out of the path of a sprinkler as they are out walking or put coins in someone else's parking meter that's just about to expire.

Come up with a list of 20 simple but kind acts that people your age might do. Think about things you could do for one another, for family members, for teachers, for bus drivers, for friends, for neighbors and for people you have never even met. (Then try actually doing some of the items on your list!)

1. _____
2. _____
3. _____
4. _____
5. _____
6. _____
7. _____
8. _____
9. _____
10. _____
11. _____
12. _____
13. _____
14. _____
15. _____
16. _____
17. _____
18. _____
19. _____
20. _____

Answer key
Kindness is catching

Answers will vary. Here are a few possibilities:

1. Send $5.00 to a brother or sister who is a college student.
2. Erase the graffiti on your desk in every class.
3. When you hear good music coming from the band room, compliment the band teacher.
4. Help the kid who always gets picked on pick up the books and papers the school bully always throws on the ground.
5. When your parents look extra tired, turn your music down before they ask.
6. Throw away the litter in the school halls.
7. Rake the neighbor's lawn.
8. Buy candy from the cute little boy selling it for his soccer team, even though you already bought three boxes from your sister.
9. Let someone else have the television remote control.
10. Put away the dishes in the dishwasher without being asked.
11. Bring your mom and/or dad breakfast in bed, for no reason at all — and clean up afterward.
12. Tell your teacher how much you like his or her class.
13. Pay for the pizza your dad ordered.
14. Leave an anonymous note for someone, telling the person how nice he or she looks today.
15. Instead of gagging and complaining, just throw away the green moldy food you find in the little container in the back of the refrigerator.
16. Let your sister borrow your nicest outfit, just to be nice.
17. Vacuum the house.
18. If you drank the last of the milk, stop and buy a gallon on your way home tonight.
19. Wear something your mom likes when you visit Grandma.
20. Don't slam your bedroom door when your parents tell you that you can't go somewhere you want to go.

March

Daisies and dandelions

Gardening, Nature and Ecology Books Month — March

In honor of Gardening, Nature and Ecology Books Month, see if you can complete the puzzle below. For each category listed along the side of the page, think of an appropriate word that begins with the letter at the top of the page. The first item is done for you.

G A R D E N

	G	A	R	D	E	N
Flowers	_geranium_					
Vegetables						
Fruits						
Trees						
Other things found in a garden						

Answers will vary. Here are some possibilities:

G A R D E N

	G	A	R	D	E	N
Flowers	geranium	azalea	rhododendron	dahlia	Easter lily	narcissus
Vegetables	garbanzo beans	acorn squash	rutabaga	dandelion greens	eggplant	new potatoes
Fruits	gooseberry	apple	raspberry	date	elderberry	nectarine
Trees	grapefruit	apricot	Russian olive	date palm	elm	Norway maple
Other things found in a garden	gazebo	ants	rake	dirt	earth worms	newts

Going hog wild

People don't often stop to think about pigs and hogs, but they are everywhere. All right, maybe you don't see pigs strolling down city streets or hanging around parking lots. But the words "pig" and "hog" occur in our language all the time. See if you can figure out the pig references in the sentences below.

Example

Claire won the lottery and started buying yachts, mansions, expensive cars and jewelry. Everyone who knew her said she had gone _____*hog wild*_____ with her money.

1. "Clean up your room!" said Eric's mother. "It looks like a _____ !"
2. Whenever the tooth fairy visited, Amy carefully put every quarter in her _____ .
3. "I am ordering ten pizzas for my slumber party," said Shaniqua. "We also have three cases of Coke, four gallons of ice cream, three bottles of chocolate syrup, two bags of nuts and three cans of whipped cream. We are really going to _____ ."
4. Christopher said, "I told him not to use that excuse. It was really a dumb idea, but he is so _____ he just wouldn't listen to me."
5. "He's no fun to play with," griped Antonio. "He always _____ the ball and won't give anyone else a chance."
6. "You didn't KNOW you weren't supposed to give a party and invite 122 people to the house while your mom and I were out of town?" cried Jesse's father. "You didn't KNOW????? That's _____ !!!"
7. Lyndsay held the baby and said, "This little _____ went to market; this little _____ stayed home."
8. Sarah's mother braided her _____ so tight that she got a headache.
9. Little Andy's parents didn't want him to repeat what they were saying about the neighbors, who were driving them crazy. That's why they spoke in _____ .
10. The state champions raced onto the field and tossed the _____ around, intimidating the members of the opposing team.
11. Mr. Yung woke up unable to move without pain. "Maybe you shouldn't have given all the grandchildren those _____ rides," said Mrs. Yung.
12. "My one true love is, of course, Kermit!" sighed Miss _____ .

Bonus

Now see if you can add 3-5 items of your own to the puzzle. Use any "pig" words not used above.

Answer key
Going hog wild

1. pigsty
2. piggy bank
3. pig out
4. pig-headed
5. hogs
6. hogwash
7. piggy; piggy
8. pigtails
9. pig Latin
10. pigskin
11. piggyback
12. Piggy

Bonus

Answers will vary. A few possibilities:

1. Daffy was disappointed at not getting invited to the wedding of *Porky and Petunia Pig*.
2. "You'd be best off with a *brick* house," advised the real estate agent. "Didn't you ever read the story *'The Three Little Pigs'*?"
3. My mom is an inventor, and she always uses me as a *guinea pig* to try out new products.
4. Slim rode up to the varmints who had been stealing his cattle. "I reckon I'm going to have to *hog-tie* all three of you and take you in to Marshall Dillon," he said.
5. My mother made *pigs in a blanket* for brunch.

Going to the dogs

In 1925, the people of Nome, Alaska (then Alaska Territory), desperately needed a serum to fight a diphtheria epidemic that threatened the town. The serum was raced from Nenana, Alaska, to Nome by dog team. Twenty teams relayed the medicine 674 miles in 127.5 hours.

In honor of this historic relay, the Iditarod Sled Dog Race is held every year, with competition starting in Anchorage on the first Saturday in March. The first team usually arrives in Nome 10-12 days later, with the rest of the teams arriving throughout the next week and a half. The race covers almost 1200 miles of rough but beautiful terrain, including mountain ranges, frozen rivers, dense forests, desolate tundra and miles of windswept coast, often at temperatures far below zero. Mushers may encounter temperature extremes of +45°F to -60°F in their long and exhausting journey.

The name "Iditarod" is believed to come from the Athabascan Indians, who called their inland hunting ground Haiditarod, "the distant place." Miners later founded a town at the hunting camp, calling it Iditarod. Eventually a trail from Nome through Iditarod and on to Seward became know as the Iditarod Trail.

Imagine that you are entering the Iditarod this year. You have 15 dogs, each carefully named because you think good names bring good luck. What are your dogs names? Explain the significance of each name.

1. _____
   _____
2. _____
   _____
3. _____
   _____
4. _____
   _____
5. _____
   _____
6. _____
   _____
7. _____

8. _____
   _____

9. _____
   _____
10. _____
    _____
11. _____
    _____
12. _____
    _____
13. _____
    _____
14. _____
    _____
15. _____
    _____

Bonus

Is entering the Iditarod a challenge that would appeal to you? Why or why not?

Answer key
Going to the dogs

Answers will vary. Here is one example:

1. Einstein — after Albert Einstein because I want my dogs to be smart.
2. Tucker — after Mrs. Tucker, my fourth grade teacher, who was my favorite.
3. Crockett — after my little brother Dave. (I always call him Davey Crockett.)
4. Ali — because I want a dog that's quick on his feet, like Muhammed Ali.
5. Trophy — because I want the dogs to be winners!
6. Comet — because I want the dogs to be fast.
7. Salsa — because salsa is hot, and I want the dogs to stay warm.
8. Mamie — after my grandmother, who thinks I'm wonderful.
9. Arnold — after Arnold Schwarzenegger because I want my dogs to be strong.
10. Crawford — after Cindy Crawford, because I want beautiful dogs.
11. Kathleen — after my best friend, who is always loyal, and I want my dogs to be loyal.
12. Marathon — because I want my dogs to have the endurance of a marathon runner.
13. Greenie — because green is my favorite color, and it brings me good luck.
14. Mocha — because mocha is my favorite kind of ice cream, and it's got coffee in it. Coffee keeps you awake, and I sure want my dogs to stay awake.
15. Kim — after the gymnast Kerri Strug, who acted for the good of her team in the Olympics. I want my dogs to be team players, too.

Bonus

If I was going to choose a competition, it sure wouldn't be the Iditarod. I really, really, really hate being cold. I've never liked ice skating or skiing very much, mostly because of the cold. My sister even complains because I like the window shut in our bedroom in the summer, just because I get a little chilly at night. I can't imagine hanging around outside very long in Alaska.

Also, I don't like being alone, and the mushers are alone (except for their dogs) a lot. I'd much rather be in some kind of team competition where I would be working with others.

Women around the world

To celebrate International Women's Day, find the correct answers to items 1-19, below. (This will require some research on your part.) Circle the first letter of each correct answer and write the letter in the space provided. The first one is completed for you, as an example.

Take the letters you have written in the spaces and fit them into the box at the bottom of this page. For example, the "H" from #1 will go above every blank with a #1 below it. When you have completed the box, you will have spelled out a quotation by a famous woman.

H 1.   Elizabeth Blackwell, the first woman doctor, is known for her medical writings on . . .

    PEDIATRICS   HYGIENE   INNOCULATIONS
    CANCER   LEECHES

_____ 2.   Nobel Prize winner Madam Curie used her knowledge of this element to organize radiological (X-ray) services during World War I:

    OXYGEN   CARBON   NEON   RADIUM   CALIFORNIUM

_____ 3.   This book by Rachel Carson examined the increasing use of chemical pesticides and herbicides, sparking controversy over the ecological state of our planet:

    THE LION KING   *SILENT SPRING*   *THE OLD MAN AND THE SEA*
    MAMA EARTH   *PESTICIDES AND YOU*

___	*H*	___	___	___		___	___	
9	1	13	2	13		14	3	

___	___	___	*H*	___	___	___
4	15	9	1	14	4	16

___	___	___	___	___	___	___	___	___	___	___
17	15	5	6	7	14	17	8	9	13	19

___	___	___	___	___
8	10	15	11	9

___	___	___	___	___	___	___	___
15	2	19	14	4	8	2	12

___	___	___	___	___	___	___	___
13	18	11	8	7	14	9	12

___	___	___	___	___		___	___	___	___
8	7	14	17	13		6	8	11	7

_____4. Author of *The Feminine Mystique*, Betty Friedan advocated changing the sexist language of classified employment ads and served as the first president of this organization:

NATIONAL ORGANIZATION FOR WOMEN (NOW)
COLLEGE REPUBLICANS
GIRL SCOUTS OF AMERICA
AMERICAN CIVIL LIBERTIES UNION (ACLU)
DAUGHTERS OF THE AMERICAN REVOLUTION (DAR)

_____5. As Minister of Education and Science, this woman, who became the first female prime minister of Great Britain, provoked a storm of protest by abolishing free milk in schools:

MARGARET THATCHER   GEORGE ELIOT   JANE AUSTEN
ANNE BOLEYN   EMMA THOMPSON

_____6. Jane Austen wrote this novel (originally titled *First Impressions*) secretly, hiding her work in a sewing basket whenever she saw someone coming:

*LITTLE WOMEN   MUCH ADO ABOUT NOTHING
PRIDE AND PREJUDICE   FRANKENSTEIN
WUTHERING HEIGHTS*

_____7. Known for her black bonnet and her fiery speeches, Mother Jones, even at the age of 93, showed up wherever there were . . .

EXECUTIONS   HOT AIR BALLOON LAUNCHES
MOVIE PREMIERS   LABOR DISPUTES   SUFFRAGIST MEETINGS

_____8. Arrested for voting (because she was a woman), this suffragist died before the passage of the 19th Amendment allowing women the right to vote:

BERNHARDT, SARAH   ANTHONY, SUSAN B.   STEINEM, GLORIA
TRUTH, SOJOURNER   MEAD, MARGARET

_____9. This U.S. citizen was convicted of treason for her radio broadcasts of disheartening propaganda to U.S. troops in the South Pacific during World War II:

DOROTHEA DIX   MARIA TALLCHIEF   ROSA PARKS
ELEANOR ROOSEVELT   TOKYO ROSE

_____10. Not allowed to fly in the United States because of her color, this woman trained as a pilot in France and became the first African-American pilot in the United States:

AMELIA EARHART   BESSIE COLEMAN   ROSA PARKS
MAE WEST   ELLA FITZGERALD

_____11. Harriet Tubman was so successful as a conductor of this that at one point there was a $40,000 reward for her capture — dead or alive:

QUAKER MEETING   SANTE FE RAILROAD   BOSTON POPS
SHERMAN'S MARCH TO THE SEA   UNDERGROUND RAILROAD

_____ 12. Known for her studies on the roles of males and females, anthropologist Margaret Mead's book *Coming of Age in Samoa* explored cultural differences among . . .

GRANDPARENTS   CHIMPANZEES   YOUNG PEOPLE
BALLROOM DANCERS   RETIRED COUPLES

_____ 13. This controversial first lady started a furniture company to help the unemployed and was instrumental in writing and passing the Declaration of Human Rights:

LADY BIRD JOHNSON   ELEANOR ROOSEVELT
MARY TODD LINCOLN   DOLLY MADISON   HILLARY CLINTON

_____ 14. Golda Meir signed this country's Declaration of Independence in 1948 and served as its prime minister from 1969-1974:

RUSSIA   ISRAEL   ENGLAND   KUWAIT
THE NETHERLANDS

_____ 15. Noted for her New Mexican landscapes and flowers, this artist wore only black and white clothing for much of her adult life:

GRANDMA MOSES   KAHLO, FRIDA   O'KEEFFE, GEORGIA
CATLETT, ELIZABETH   CASSATT, MARY

_____ 16. Her unofficial role as confidante to her father (India's first prime minister) prepared her for her position as Prime Minister of India:

MEIR, GOLDA   GANDHI, INDIRA   THATCHER, MARGARET
MARCOS, IMELDA   PERON, EVA

_____ 17. After her husband, Peter III, was overthrown by the Imperial Guard, this woman became the leader of Russia and greatly expanded its empire:

CATHERINE THE GREAT   ANNE BOLEYN   QUEEN ISABELLA
ANASTASIA   ANNA KARENINA

_____ 18. This daughter of Anne Boleyn and Henry VIII became the ruler of a powerful country at the age of 22:

QUEEN ELIZABETH I   CATHERINE THE GREAT   CLEOPATRA
MARY QUEEN OF SCOTS   MARIE ANTOINETTE

_____ 19. This medieval author produced more than 20 distinguished works, including *The Medieval Woman's Mirror of Honor*, becoming the first professional woman writer in France:

WOLLSTONECRAFT, MARY   DE PIZAN, CHRISTINE
STEIN, GERTRUDE   BERNHARDT, SARAH   FRIEDAN, BETTY

Answer key
Women around the world

1. HYGIENE
2. RADIUM
3. *SILENT SPRING*
4. NATIONAL ORGANIZATION FOR WOMEN
5. MARGARET THATCHER
6. *PRIDE AND PREJUDICE*
7. LABOR DISPUTES
8. ANTHONY, SUSAN B.
9. TOKYO ROSE
10. BESSIE COLEMAN
11. UNDERGROUND RAILROAD
12. YOUNG PEOPLE
13. ELEANOR ROOSEVELT
14. ISRAEL
15. O'KEEFFE, GEORGIA
16. GANDHI, INDIRA
17. CATHERINE THE GREAT
18. QUEEN ELIZABETH I
19. DE PIZAN, CHRISTINE

> There is nothing complicated about ordinary equality.
> Alice Paul

What a yawn

Most Boring Films of the Year Awards Day

The "Most Boring Films of the Year" awards are announced the second Monday in March by an organization called The Boring Institute. If you were able to vote for the award, what movie would you pick? What if you were able to go beyond boring and pick the all-around *worst* movie? What movie would you pick?

Imagine that you are a film critic like Gene Siskel or Roger Ebert, writing for a newspaper. Write a short review of the worst movie you have ever seen.

Getting started

Jot down some notes about the movie you have chosen. Why did you hate it?

1. To make your opinion convincing, you will have to give your readers reasons why this particular movie is so bad. For example, the characters might be shallow or unconvincing, or the plot about as deep as a mud puddle. Maybe a film that promised "action-packed adventure" left you snoring in your seat. Some areas you might consider are character development, plot, setting, costumes, acting, believability and special effects.

2. Whenever you make a point, be sure to back it up with at least one detail from the movie. For example, if you say that the characters don't sound realistic when they speak, you might quote the hero when he says, "My darling Rebecca, light of my life, I cherish you a great deal and hope that perhaps we might intertwine our respective lives and create a future together."

3. Finally, try to give your review a snappy headline that will make people want to read your story. For example, if you hated the movie *Waterworld*, your title might be "*Waterworld* is all dried up." (Note: Remember to underline or italicize the title of the movie. Also, newspapers generally capitalize only the first word of a headline.)

Answer key
What a yawn

Answers will vary. Here are three examples written by students:

Waterworld is a washout

Waterworld is not worth its fifteen billion dollar price tag. It isn't even worth a $3.00 video rental charge. While the concept is interesting (The surface of a futuristic Earth is covered with water as a result of the ice caps melting), the movie itself just doesn't float.

The set and the costumes are strange enough to keep your interest for the first 10 minutes. (Kevin Costner's character has webbed feet.) However, the plot moves at a pace slower than evolution itself. And if you are looking for any depth, you'll have to be satisfied with the water. You won't find it in the characters, who act like stereotypes from the 1950s, even though they are living in a world of the future. At one point, Costner's character actually breathes air (and life) into a helpless female, despite his earlier intention of selling her to a pirate. That doesn't make much sense, of course, but neither does this movie. Plan on needing resuscitation if you see *Waterworld*.

Elizabeth D.

The writing of the green

All over the country, cities celebrate Saint Patrick's Day by putting on parades with bands, floats, cars, motorcycles and lots of people — all wearing green.

Imagine that you are watching a Saint Patrick's Day parade and something strange, exciting or very unusual starts to happen. Write about what happens. However, to celebrate the wearing of the gr**ee**n, use as many words as possible with **ee** in them. See if you can use at least 25 **ee** words in your story. (Be sure you use words with **ee**, not **ea**. The two are easily confused.)

Here is a list of 40 words you may choose from. However, feel free to use any other **ee** words not listed, including names and places with **ee**.

List of **ee** words:

1. freedom	11. deem	21. degree	31. three
2. tree	12. careen	22. deep	32. fee
3. bleed	13. spleen	23. speech	33. flee
4. preen	14. heel	24. speed	34. esteem
5. greet	15. feel	25. weed	35. green
6. knee	16. steep	26. weep	36. wee
7. seen	17. steer	27. weevil	37. heed
8. decree	18. steel	28. tee	38. glee
9. creek	19. reel	29. bee	39. agree
10. reek	20. reef	30. gee	40. deer

Answer key
The writing of the green

Answers will vary. Here is one possibility:

Sleep. I **needed sleep**. "Wake up, Janie," my mom **screeched** from downstairs. "The parade starts in an hour."

"Just **fifteen** more minutes, Mom. Then I'll get up," I pleaded, surprised I still had the power of **speech**.

"I warned you not to stay up until **three**. What were you thinking?"

Instead of answering, I pulled myself out from under the **sheets**. This was **sheer** agony, but somehow I managed. According to my little brother Patrick, we **needed** to get there early because the **streets** would be packed. I'm not sure why we all respected the authority of a seven-year-old. Maybe it was because he is the family fanatic when it comes to Saint Patrick's Day — for obvious reasons. In any case, Patrick was right. When we had finally hiked up the **steep**, hilly **street** where we had had to park, the sidewalks were **teeming** with excited Irish-**wannabees** with shamrocks on their **cheeks**.

Before I knew what was happening, my own **cheeks** were being violently **squeezed** by a large woman I didn't recognize. "Little Janie Connor! I haven't seen you since you were **knee-high** to a grasshopper. You're just growing like a **weed**, aren't you? You remember me, don't you? I'm Stuart **Meeber**'s mother." Before I could react to being compared to undesirable plant life, Stuart **Meeber** himself was in my face. What a **geek**! Stuart was in my homeroom a couple of years ago, in sixth grade, I think. When he moved across town in the middle of the year, no one in our class was exactly **weeping,** if you know what I mean.

"**Gee**, fancy **meeting** you here. How have you **been**?"

"Fine," I said, with no great **degree** of enthusiasm. I felt trapped, surrounded by **cheering** people. There was no **fleeing**.

Stuart's breath **reeked**, and he kept attempting conversation. "Guess what I had for breakfast?"

"**Leeks**?"

"No, **green** waffles. My dad makes them every St. Pat's Day," he said, looking at me as though *I* was the weird one. I was slightly **peeved** at his attitude.

Thankfully, the parade was starting, and I didn't have to talk to him any more. A few bands marched by, and then some horses. (After that they had to **sweep**.) Then came the fifty-foot leprechaun balloon. Floating twenty **feet** above Main **Street,** it made the humans **steering** it with their tethers look like the *real* leprechauns.

Suddenly the seam on its right **knee** burst open, and the balloon was **careening** down the hill, **speeding** toward Garcia's **Screen** Door Factory. The whole crowd **kneeled,** covering their heads. I, of course, kept an even **keel**. The factory was made of **steel**, so it's not like a balloon could knock it over or anything. Stuart, though, was clearly losing it. "What if the leprechaun crashes down on those people? What are we going to do? Oh no, I **feel** sick. I **feel** really sick!"

"**Geez,** Stuart. Calm down," I said. "There's no **need** to go off the **deep** end. It's not like a balloon is heavy enough to **squeeze** the life out of anyone."

There was no need for my consolations, however. After narrowly missing the factory, the fifty-foot leprechaun soared into the park. By then it was so limp it just landed softly on the grass, where it was quietly inspected by the **geese**.

Stuart recovered.

Brynn P.

Under the weather

Everyone is interested in the weather. No matter where we are or what we are doing, the weather affects our mood, our choices, our plans and more.

The weather is so important, in fact, that it has invaded our language. Weather-related words and phrases turn up everywhere. Here are a number of them:

1. Don't **rain** on my parade.
2. She was feeling under the **weather**.
3. Every **cloud** has a silver lining.
4. He has a **sunny** disposition.
5. **Lightning** never strikes twice.
6. Tears fell like **rain**.
7. They received a **frosty** reception.
8. He gave an **icy** stare.
9. The bad news **dampened** their spirits.
10. The speaker was long-**winded**.
11. It was probably the calm before the **storm**.
12. His voice was as cold as **ice**.
13. The situation **snowballed** out of control.
14. She was as fast as greased **lightning**.
15. We saw the **thundering** herd in the distance.
16. The program brought a **flood** of mail.
17. It looks like a **tornado** hit this room.
18. The **heat** is on in the final days of this campaign.
19. The bride-to-be was going to a wedding **shower**.
20. She walks around in a **fog**.

Choose three of the phrases above and interpret them in sketches. Use your imagination. Here are two examples:

He gave an **icy** stare.

He has a **sunny** disposition.

Bonus

See if you can add at least five weather examples to the list above.

1. _____
2. _____
3. _____
4. _____
5. _____

Answer key
Under the weather

Answers will vary. Here are some possibilities:

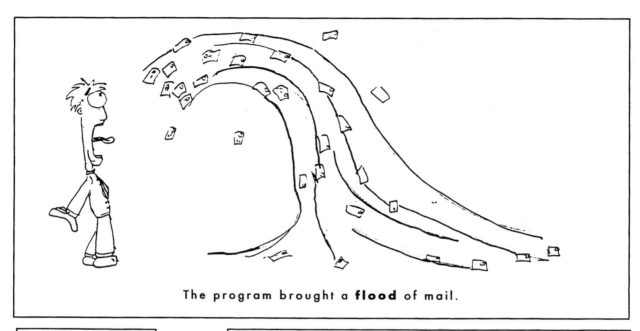

The program brought a **flood** of mail.

His voice was as cold as **ice**.

The situation **snowballed** out of control.

Bonus

Answers will vary. Here are some possibilities:

1. She's just a little ray of **sunshine**, isn't she?
2. He was in and out of the office like a **whirlwind**.
3. He ran like the **wind**.
4. She just **breezed** by me.
5. We sure **snowed** him.

April

How much is that doggie in the window?

In honor of Dog Appreciation Month, imagine some new breeds of dog. Suppose you crossed a Doberman pinscher with a poodle. You would have a *doodle*. Or imagine crossing a Pomeranian with a Chihuahua. You would have a *Pomehuahua*.

Name the new breed you would get if you mixed the breeds of dog listed below. (And, yes, there is more than one answer possible for each combination. Choose the combination you like best.)

1. dingo and Great Dane _____
2. schnauzer and husky _____
3. Labrador and beagle _____
4. poodle and schnauzer _____
5. Saint Bernard and Great Dane _____
6. dingo and Doberman _____
7. collie and Saint Bernard _____
8. malamute and mutt _____
9. Chihuahua and poodle _____
10. boxer and sheep dog _____

Bonus

Add five more combinations to the list above. Here are a few breeds of dog you might consider: rottweiler, Irish setter, Dalmatian, terrier, sheep dog, Yorkshire terrier (yorkie), boxer, bulldog, mastiff, Afghan hound, cocker spaniel, basset hound, Maltese, chow, Pekinese, Sharpei, greyhound, collie, sheltie, whippet, Weimaraner, bloodhound, pit bull.

11. _____
12. _____
13. _____
14. _____
15. _____

Super bonus

Find a dog joke to share.

Example:

Why did the cowboy get a dachshund (wiener dog)?
Because he wanted to get a long little doggie.

Answer key
How much is that doggie in the window?

Answers will vary. Here are some possibilities:

1. dingo and Great Dane: ding Dane
2. schnauzer and husky: schnusky
3. Labrador and beagle: Leagle
4. poodle and schnauzer: poozer or schnoodle
5. Saint Bernard and Great Dane: Saint Dane
6. dingo and Doberman: dingman
7. collie and Saint Bernard: collard
8. Malamute and mutt: malamutt
9. Chihuahua and poodle: Chihoodle
10. boxer and sheep dog: box dog

Bonus

Answers will vary. Here are some possibilities:

11. bulldog and collie: bullie
12. cocker spaniel and Dalmatian: cockermatian
13. basset hound and terrier: basseterrier
14. Afghan hound and mutt: Afghutt
15. bloodhound and whippet: blippet

Super bonus

Answers will vary. Here is one example:

What did the three-legged dog say when he walked into the saloon?
"I'm lookin' for the man who shot my paw."

See the USA in your Chevrolet

In honor of Travel and Entertainment Books Month, get out a U.S. road atlas, travel books or pamphlets and your imagination. See if you can complete the following:

Trip #1. You and your friends decide to go to a spectacular festival held each year in October. You get in your car parked in your garage in Minneapolis, Minnesota, and go south on I-35. Next you will need to go west on I-70. In what city will you find I-70 intersecting I-35?

(1) _____

Traveling along, you know you will need to go south again in Denver. What interstate will you take in Denver in order to go south? (2) _____

Your final destination is the city where I-40 and I-25 intersect. What city and state are you in? (3) _____

Now, find out what high-flying, colorful festival takes place here each October:

(4) _____

Trip #2. You are a big sports fan and decide to visit the Pro Football Hall of Fame and the Baseball Hall of Fame. In what cities are these two attractions located?

(5) _____

(6) _____

Trip #3. Your favorite Aunt Gabby has invited you to attend the New Orleans Jazz and Heritage Festival. Aunt Gabby is expecting you at her home in New Orleans on April 30. You will be driving from your home in Idaho Falls, Idaho. Using a road atlas, plot your trip.

Write your travel itinerary, using your own paper. What day will you need to leave to get there on time? What roads will you take? Where will you stop for lunch? Where will you stop each night? (Note: Your car has a special speedometer that won't let you go more than 65 mph, and you can't spend more than 10 hours per day in the car.)

Answer key
See the USA in your Chevrolet

Trip #1

1. Kansas City, Missouri
2. I-25
3. Albuquerque, New Mexico
4. Albuquerque Hot Air Balloon Festival

Trip #2

1. Pro Football — Canton, Ohio
2. Pro Baseball — Cooperstown, New York

Trip #3

3. Answers will vary, but here is one possibility:

Day 1
April 27:   Take Interstate 15 from Idaho Falls south to Ogden, Utah, where you will connect with Interstate 80. Take I-80 east to Cheyenne, Wyoming. Stop for lunch in Evanston, Wyoming. Stay overnight in Cheyenne.

Day 2
April 28:   Take Interstate 25 south from Cheyenne to Denver. In Denver take Interstate 70 east. Stop for lunch in Goodland, Kansas. In Salina, Kansas, take Interstate 135 south to Wichita, Kansas, where you will stay overnight.

Day 3
April 29:   Take Interstate 35 out of Wichita and go south to Dallas, where you will have lunch (a big steak and Texas toast . . .) and connect with Interstate 20 east. Take I-20 east to Monroe, Louisiana, where you will stay for the night.

Day 4
April 30:   Continue on I-20 east to Jackson, Mississippi. Then go south on Interstate 55, which goes around Lake Pontchartrain and connects with Interstate 10 into New Orleans.

How many? How much?

In honor of Math Education Month, complete the problem below, using all the people in the room.

1. Take the number of pairs of feet _____

2. Subtract the total number of shoes that have the word "Nike" on them _____

3. Add the number of pierced ears _____

4. Divide by the number of people who have dark brown or black hair _____

5. Add the number of rings worn _____

6. Add the number of pairs of glasses _____

7. Subtract the number of pairs of contact lenses _____

8. Multiply by the number of people who have a birthday in February _____

9. Divide by the number of people whose last names begin with T or M _____

10. Add the number of watches worn on the left wrist_____

The answer: _____

Bonus

Now create your own eight-step problem for the group to solve. (Be sure to include a separate page with the correct answer.) Have some fun designing an interesting challenge.

Answer key
How many? How much?

Bonus

Answers will vary. Here is one example:

1. Take the number of steps it takes to walk all the way around the school.
2. Divide by the number of adults who work in the school library or media center.
3. Multiply by the cost of a carton of milk in the cafeteria.
4. Subtract the number of pounds of sugar the home economics teacher has on hand at school.
5. Add your teacher's height in inches.
6. Add the number of boys' and girls' restrooms in the school.
7. Subtract the number of minutes in the normal school day.
8. Multiply by the number of years the principal has been the principal at your school.

What's so funny?

All 18 words below are synonyms of the word *laugh*. Define each — using either a dictionary or your common sense.

Next, rate each of the words below according to degree, from weakest to strongest. (In your opinion, which word shows the strongest form of laughter? Give that word an "18." Give the weakest form a "1.")

_____ laugh _____

_____ cackle _____

_____ chortle _____

_____ chuckle _____

_____ giggle _____

_____ snicker _____

_____ twitter _____

_____ guffaw _____

_____ belly laugh _____

_____ roar _____

_____ howl _____

_____ grin _____

_____ smirk _____

_____ smile _____

_____ crack up _____

_____ roll in the aisles _____

_____ be in stitches _____

_____ shriek _____

Now that you have rated these words, write a story that includes all of them. The catch is that you have to include the words in the order you rated them (or in the reverse order). Also, keep the story to less than one page. Good luck!

Answer key
What's so funny?

Answers will vary. Here is one example:

1. grin: to turn up the sides of your mouth and show your teeth
2. smile: to turn up the sides of your mouth
3. smirk: a smile with an attitude
4. twitter: a light, joyous laugh often done while speaking
5. snicker: an inside laugh when your mouth is closed
6. giggle: a small nervous laugh usually done in groups
7. chuckle: a laugh that says, "Everything's okay."
8. chortle: a laugh that says, "Everything is great."
9. laugh: the basic sound made by happy people
10. cackle: a devious laugh
11. guffaw: a loud burst of laughter
12. crack up: when you start losing control with laughter
13. howl: a sound that comes from laughing so hard you sound like an animal
14. roar: a big booming, animal-like laugh
15. shriek: a laugh so hard you can't control the way it sounds
16. belly laugh: a deep, hard laugh that comes from the bottom of your tummy
17. be in stitches: to laugh so hard your sides hurt
18. roll in the aisles: falling down and physically out-of-control laughter

Homicide investigators Ramona Ramirez and Tony Caporricci were driving around in a squad car. The circus was in town, but not much else was happening in Cheesy Town, Wisconsin. Suddenly they heard the radio dispatcher, LaVerne.

"I thought you two might be bored," she said. "So I'm calling to tell you a joke that my six-year-old told me yesterday: What time is it when an elephant sits on a fence?"

"What time?" Ramona asked with a sigh.

"Time to get the fence fixed," LaVerne answered. "Hey, why aren't you guys laughing?"

"I was about six years old the first time I heard that joke too, LaVerne," Tony explained.

"Wait a minute . . . I have a call coming in . . . You two are to get to the Big Top immediately. There has been a death. Murder is suspected."

Ramona and Tony sped down Cheddar Avenue to the Dairy Festival Fairgrounds, where the circus was being held. As they came to a screeching halt, they saw a crowd of people outside the big top tent. Beside it, there was an elephant on top of what used to be a fence. Out from underneath the elephant was a long coarse beard. (They later learned that it belonged to the bearded lady, Georgeanne Lynderapolis.)

Remembering LaVerne's joke, Ramona kept looking at the ground, trying to conceal the **grin** on her face. Tony had his hand over his mouth to cover his big **smile**. Then Tony glanced over at Ramona with an obvious **smirk** on his face and she began to **twitter**. Next thing everyone knew Ramona and Tony started to **snicker**. Together they tried to suppress a **giggle**, but Tony let out a **chuckle** forcing Ramona to **chortle**.

The audience was stunned at the homicide investigators' behavior, but the harder the two tried to stop **laughing,** the louder they **cackled**. Finally with a loud **guffaw**, Ramona said, "It's time to get the fence fixed."

By this time, Police Chief Wycoski came on the scene with the murder suspect, Wayne Wedel the elephant trainer, in tow. He demanded to know what was going on, but it was too late. The two had officially **cracked up**. The exasperated face on Wayne Wedel only made them laugh harder. Ramona was **howling**, and Tony was **roaring**. The angry face on Wycoski only made it worse. When he tried to say something, Ramona just **shrieked** and Tony let out peals of **belly laughter**. By the time the two **were in stitches**, Wayne Wedel couldn't take it anymore. He screamed, "I finally do something big and noteworthy in this world, and these two homicide investigators are **rolling in the aisles**. I'm guilty, OK. She dumped me, and I was heartbroken. So I trained Daphne the elephant to sit on the fence that Georgeanne always took a nap under. So, yes, indirectly I killed Georgeanne Lynderapolis." After this, Wedel confessed the whole story.

Ramona and Tony stopped laughing long enough to book him.

Luisa M.

F a c t   o r   n o t ?

Because April Fools' Day is traditionally a day of jokes, pranks and practical jokes, people must be on guard all day long. If someone comes up and stares at your head with a look of horror and says, "Is that a tarantula in your hair?" it's probably best not to scream or pass out from terror. If you do, you're likely to hear, "April Fool!" when you open your eyes.

Here's some practice in judging the truth of what you hear. Below are 75 statements about all kinds of things, both trivial and important. See if you can judge the truth of each statement. Place a "true" or a "false" beside each item. (Be careful. Some of the answers may surprise you.)

_____ 1. Tornadoes seldom move at speeds greater than 40 miles per hour.

_____ 2. Colorado is the biggest Rocky Mountain state.

_____ 3. Tomatoes are considered vegetables.

_____ 4. The Sea of Tranquillity is a small sea in West Africa.

_____ 5. Large kangaroos can cover over 60 feet in one jump.

_____ 6. Truth or Consequences, New Mexico, was named after the television game show Truth or Consequences.

_____ 7. Synchronized swimming was an event at the first modern Olympics held in Athens, Greece, in 1896.

_____ 8. The first minimum wage in the United States was 25 cents per hour.

_____ 9. Pasta originated in Asia and was brought to Italy from China by Marco Polo.

_____ 10. Tapping your fingernails makes your nails grow faster.

_____ 11. Nevada has a highway specifically for UFO landings.

_____ 12. Later in life, Benjamin Franklin kept a tamed bear as a pet. Everyone called the bear Gentle Ben.

_____ 13. George Eliot is the man who wrote the books *Silas Marner* and *Middlemarch*.

_____ 14. Identical twins have the same fingerprints.

_____ 15. No one in the musical group "Hootie and the Blowfish" is actually named Hootie or Blowfish.

_____ 16. Eating too many carrots can cause a person to turn orange.

_____ 17. The first elevator was erected in 1743 in the Palace of Versailles.

_____ 18. Saturn is the third largest planet after Jupiter and Neptune.

_____ 19. The shortest building in the world is the Lego Building in downtown Houston, Texas.

_____ 20. Button Gwinnet was the first person to sign the Constitution of the United States.

_____ 21. The poet Shel Silverstein also wrote the song "A Boy Named Sue," recorded by Johnny Cash.

_____ 22. Nobody doesn't like Sara Lee.

_____ 23. Pocahontas was pictured on the back of the 1875 $20 bill.

_____ 24. "Counterclockwise" refers to the direction a clock's hands appear to be moving if you sit on the kitchen counter and look over your left shoulder at the clock.

_____ 25. If you multiply any number by zero, the answer is one half of that number.

_____ 26. If you get too close to a porcupine, it is likely to shoot its needles at you.

_____ 27. There are approximately 140 calories in a can of Coca-Cola.

_____ 28. Glass is made from sand.

_____ 29. Computer viruses are spread by touching a computer's parallel port with un-washed hands.

_____ 30. One out of 40 people is a redhead.

_____ 31. Eating the leaves of the poinsettia plant is usually fatal.

_____ 32. A baby pig is called a pigglita.

_____ 33. The week of the first Monday of June is National Bathroom Reading Week, which promotes reading and learning in the bathroom.

_____ 34. It is illegal to pray in American public schools.

_____ 35. Polyester is harvested from the fur of tropical-dwelling polyps.

_____ 36. The first crossword puzzle book was published in 1924.

_____ 37. The capital of North Dakota is Fargo.

_____ 38. The best-selling flavor of Ben and Jerry's ice cream is Cherry Garcia.

_____ 39. The first instrument given to Beatle John Lennon as a child was the accordion.

_____ 40. The first World Series was held in 1930.

_____ 41. The covering on the end of a shoe lace is called an aglet.

_____ 42. The Baby Ruth candybar was named for a baseball player.

_____ 43. Albuquerque, New Mexico, is known as the Mile High City.

_____ 44. M&Ms were invented by two men whose names began with "M."

_____ 45. An airplane's Black Box is really orange.

_____ 46. The longest hiccuping attack lasted 65 years.

_____ 47. Panama hats are made in Panama.

_____ 48. Baby ostriches have been known to eat small kittens.

_____ 49. Big Ben is the name of a large clock in London.

_____ 50. Speaking before a group is among the top five fears of U.S. residents.

_____ 51. The dancer Fred Astaire had insurance for his feet.

_____ 52. A group of ferrets is called a business.

_____ 53. A group of crows is called a murder.

_____ 54. Over 850,000 people threw up after riding Disneyland's Magic Mountain roller coaster in 1993.

_____ 55. The black mamba, an African snake, has been said to move up to 30 mph while chasing a man on horseback.

_____ 56. Frequently chewing the bark of the Australian Sycamore can cause a human or other primate's hair to fall out.

_____ 57. The first toothbrushes originated in China and were made of hogs' hair.

_____ 58. In 1981, the United Nations declared spaghetti the official international food.

_____ 59. Experts predict the world's population will be 12 billion by the year 2050.

_____ 60. You must have a special musician's license to sell electric guitars in the state of Maine.

_____ 61. A wallaby is an Australian land form unique to mountain ranges over 5500 feet in elevation.

_____ 62. The capybara is the world's largest rodent, weighing up to 174 pounds.

_____ 63. In Portugal and Chile, a six-pack of soft drinks always contains eight cans.

_____ 64. One of the categories for the Grammy Awards is Best Polka Album.

_____ 65. Diamonds cannot burn.

_____ 66. "Musophobia" means "fear of loud music."

_____ 67. One effective way to quiet a dog is to sprinkle grape juice over it.

_____ 68. Broccoli is a good source of calcium.

_____ 69. More sandals are imported into the U.S. from Tonga than from any other country.

_____ 70. Infants who squeeze an adult's finger are more likely to read at a younger age.

_____ 71. The tango originated on the island of Tahiti, where native men would strut forward and then backward in imitation of a male toucan.

_____ 72. Most trees actually grow faster if they have a tire swing hanging from one of their branches.

_____ 73. Daikon is the only vegetable that can be grown in Greenland.

_____ 74. The Great Red Spot, a storm on Jupiter, is larger than the Earth.

_____ 75. The continental shelf is a cabinet in the United Nations Building in Geneva, Switzerland.

Answer key
Fact or not?

1. True.
2. False. The biggest is Montana.
3. False. They are considered fruits.
4. False. It is a crater on the moon.
5. False. They can, however, cover more than 30 feet with one jump.
6. True.
7. True.
8. True. It was instituted in 1938.
9. True.
10. True. Tapping stimulates cell growth.
11. True. Nevada State Route 375 was renamed the Extraterrestrial Highway in 1996.
12. False.
13. False. George Eliot was the pen name of a *woman*, Mary Ann Evans, who did write these novels.
14. False.
15. True. The South Carolina band has four members: Dean Felber, Mark Bryan, Darius Rucker and Jim "Soni" Sonefeld.
16. True. Extremely high levels of beta carotine have been known to turn the skin orange.
17. True. It operated through the use of weights.
18. False. Saturn is the second largest planet. (Jupiter is the largest.)
19. False.
20. True.
21. True.
22. False. Lots of people prefer other desserts.
23. True.
24. False.

25. False. Any number multiplied by zero will always equal zero.
26. False.
27. True.
28. True. Glass is usually made of three components, one of which is silica, in the form of sand.
29. False.
30. True.
31. False. In 1975 the U.S. Consumer Product Safety Commission determined that poinsettia leaf consumption may cause discomfort, but not death.
32. False. It is called a piglet.
33. True.
34. False. Individual silent prayer in school is always legal.
35. False.
36. True.
37. False. It is Bismarck.
38. True.
39. True.
40. False. The first World Series was held 27 years earlier in 1903.
41. True.
42. False. It was named for Ruth Cleveland, oldest daughter of President Grover Cleveland.
43. False. Denver, Colorado, is the Mile High City.
44. True. They were invented by Mr. Mars and Mr. Merrie for soldiers so they could eat chocolate without getting their trigger fingers sticky.
45. True.
46. True.
47. False. They have always been made in Ecuador, though they were at one time distributed through Panama.

48. False.
49. False. It is a 13.5-ton bell in the clock tower of England's Houses of Parliament.
50. True.
51. True. Astaire's feet were insured for $650,000.
52. True.
53. True.
54. False.
55. True.
56. False.
57. True. Nylon bristles were not developed until 1938.
58. False. It has not declared an international food.
59. True.
60. False.
61. False. A wallaby is an Australian marsupial generally smaller than a kangaroo.
62. True. Also called the water hog, it is native to South America and can get up to 4'6" in length.
63. False.
64. True.
65. False. Diamonds will burn if heated to between 1400 and 1607° Fahrenheit.
66. False. Musophobia is the fear of mice.
67. False.
68. True.
69. False.
70. False.
71. False.
72. False.
73. False. Daikon is not even a vegetable.
74. True.
75. False. The continental shelf is an underwater ridge around the coastline of the world's oceans.

The legendary YOU

Perhaps you have seen a Shakespearean play. Perhaps you haven't. Either way, you probably know something about William Shakespeare — maybe even more than you *think* you know.

You probably know that he was a writer, and you probably even know that he wrote *Romeo and Juliet* and *Hamlet.* You have probably seen pictures of him. You probably even know some of his lines, like, "O Romeo! Romeo! wherefore art thou Romeo?" or, "To be, or not to be: that is the question."

No one knows exactly when Shakespeare was born, although he was baptized April 26, 1564. Even though he has been dead for almost 400 years, he is still a pretty popular guy. His 37 plays are still performed frequently all over the world. Today he is known as the greatest playwright of the English language.

Of course, while he lived Shakespeare probably didn't know that he was going to become such a legend. At the time, he probably thought he was just doing his job, which happened to be writing plays. It turns out he was awfully good at his job.

The legendary you

Today one of the simple tools we use for keeping historical information about famous people is the encyclopedia. The encyclopedia includes at least the basic facts about a famous individual, as well as *why* that person is famous. (What did he or she do to be remembered? What were his or her accomplishments? If the person didn't have accomplishments, what happened to make him or her famous?)

Imagine that it is 400 years from now. One of the famous people to be included in encyclopedias of the future is *you.* Write the encyclopedia entry about the legendary you. Here are some questions to consider:

- What are the basics about this person — birthplace, birth date, original name, etc.?
- What did the person do to be remembered 400 years from now? What were his or her accomplishments? How did he or she contribute to society?
- What is most interesting or unusual about this person?

████████████████████████████

Answers will vary. Here is one example:

Masterstefano, Rosa (1973-2100). International dancer and choreographer. Born in Rocky Ford, Colorado.

Rosa Masterstefano revolutionized the international dance scene. By the end of the 1900s, dance worldwide had hit an all-time historical low, especially among the younger generation. The most prevalent form of dance among this generation, made popular by MTV dance party shows, was an aimless kind of dance that lacked skill and rhythm. It consisted of merely planting your feet firmly on the ground, swaying your hips and flailing your arms above your head.

Masterstefano changed all this with her simple observation, "We just need new dances." She set out to create new dances that fit her generation, and she was very successful. She began by combining old dances from many different cultures with current music trends, creating something entirely new. The most popular dance she developed carried her name, Masterstefano. The Masterstefano was a combination of mambo, polka and swing.

The new dance craze quickly swept the globe. A new subculture of dancers, who called themselves the Rosies, became known for their spontaneous, all-night dance parties. Masterstefano dance studios cropped up in every big city and many small towns. Masterstefano made sure that any studio that carried her name would remain inexpensive so that anyone could learn to dance.

Her most important contribution to dance can be summed up in her own words: "Steps and moves are a significant part of dance, but dance is 90% attitude. I hope to encourage this attitude and spread enthusiasm for dance all over the world." And that she did. Even after 400 years, Masterstefano's dances are still performed by young people everywhere. Some of her dances that are still popular today are the Rosa-Rosa, the Cali Bell, the Wild Strawberry and the Spaghetti Twirl.

Masterstefano danced until her death on the day after her 127th birthday, September 23, 2100.

Rosa M.

Money doesn't grow on trees

People (often parents) say, "Money doesn't grow on trees." That's true, but wouldn't it be nice if it *did*? Or what if a tree could grow candy bars, new clothes, cars or soft drinks?

National Arbor Day recognizes the importance of trees. (In case you're wondering, an "arbor" is a shady garden shelter.) In its honor, imagine that you are a famous botanist developing a new kind of tree — a tree that grows whatever *you* think would be a good idea. Imagine your tree. Then design an advertisement for it, including a picture of the tree and your advertising copy.

Be sure to think about the audience for your ad. Do you want to sell the tree to a plant nursery, motel chains, the Forestry Service, the average gardener, the general public or another specific group? Write your ad to appeal to the audience you have chosen.

Here is one example:

The CD Tree

You don't have to go to expensive record stores or join troublesome CD clubs anymore. If you are a music lover, the CD Tree is the only thing you will need. Every week compact discs from your favorite musicians actually bloom on the CD Tree. The CDs are so new that some are not even in record stores yet.

Even if you don't have a green thumb, you can care for the CD Tree. All you need to do is keep it hidden in your dark bedroom and moisten it often with your favorite brand of cola.

Buy the CD Tree today!
For $55 (the cost of 3 CDs),
you can have an endless supply of music.

Answers will vary. Here is one possibility:

Odor No More Tree

Eliminate odors just about anywhere with the miracle leaves of the Odor No More Tree. This attractive tree has leaves that are actually useful. When you rake up these sweet-smelling leaves in the fall, you will want to save every one!

Just a few uses for the leaves:

- Have a bowlful handy when your dog comes in from the rain
- Sprinkle them on broccoli to make it more palatable
- Put a whole branch of them in your gym locker
- Munch on them for sweet-smelling breath
- Crumble a few leaves in your shoes
- Mix leaves in with the cat litter
- Mix them in the diaper pail

Only **$8.95** per foot

Do you live near a garbage dump? A feed lot? A zoo? Ask about quantity discounts. Buy a whole forest of trees, and enjoy sitting outside on your deck once more.

"We were ready to give away our beloved cats until we sprinkled dried Odor No More leaves on our carpet. Now there is no more odor from unfortunate accidents. Odor No More leaves really work!"
Herbert and Betty Keller, Pleasant Falls, Oregon

May

A spear a day keeps the doctor away?

National Asparagus Month — May

Asparagus is a vegetable that generates strong opinions. To some, it is a delicious delicacy. To others, it is an abomination that makes them gag just to think of it.

Whatever your opinion, May is the time to give asparagus some attention. In honor of National Asparagus Month, complete the following story, filling in the blanks with words that can be made from the letters in the word *asparagus*. Each letter can be used only as many times at it appears in *asparagus*.

Leon sat down to dinner. "Please (1)_____ the potatoes," he said. Leon loved potatoes. As his brother passed him the bowl, Leon looked inside and let out a (2)_____. "They are green!" he cried. "They are as green as (3)_____!"

"It's asparagus," smiled his mother. "I decided on a special treat for tonight."

Leon's spirits began to (4)_____. He loved potatoes, not asparagus. He tried to figure out what to do. He saw there was a (5)_____ where the table leaves didn't quite come together. He thought of dropping the asparagus there. He knew his mother would notice the asparagus on the floor, though.

He looked down at a spear. "Maybe I could (6)_____ it and toss it over to my sister's plate," he thought. But he knew his dad was bound to notice flying asparagus.

Finally, he looked at the little bowl in the middle of the table, next to the cream. He got an idea. "I'll cover my asparagus with (7)_____," he thought. "That is bound to make it taste good."

Sure enough, when Leon tasted the asparagus, he found it sweet and delicious. "I've always hated it," he thought. "In fact, everyone I know, except my mom, thinks it's a terrible vegetable. Now I see that asparagus has gotten a bad (8)_____. Covered with enough (9)_____, it's really delicious."

He smiled as he munched. "Now I feel happy (10)_____ a clam!" he thought.

Then he frowned. "Oops. I forgot that I hate clams." He looked over at the (11) _____bowl again. "Well, maybe I know a way to make clams taste better too!"

Bonus

After you have identified the nine words from the story above, list them here: _____

_____

_____

Write a paragraph or a short story (one page or less), using all the words above, plus the word *asparagus* and any other words you can make from those letters. One more thing — your story can't take place at the dinner table.

Good luck!

Answer key
A spear a day keeps the doctor away?

1. pass
2. gasp
3. grass
4. sag
5. gap
6. grasp
7. sugar
8. rap
9. sugar
10. as
11. sugar

Bonus

Answers will vary. Here is one example:

I've had this **gap** as wide as a stalk of **asparagus** between my two front teeth ever since I can remember. My mom swears that my dentist put it there when I was three years old, but the truth is she just doesn't like to admit that it came from her side of the family. They all have bad teeth. They're in and out of the dentist's office so much that they've had to install a turnstile. At least that's what my grandpa says. I never know when he's pulling my leg, though — or "pulling my teeth," **as** he likes to say.

He told me about this time he went to Dr. Paine to have his sweet tooth removed. He said he was through with candy once and for all. I guess Dr. Paine thought the whole thing was silly, but he let Grandpa come in anyway. "He tried to scare me with the size of that needle," Grandpa said, "and he expected my determination to **sag**. Well, I let out a little **gasp** just to humor him, but then I told him to go ahead with the shot. I wasn't going to **pass** out or anything. As it turned out, it was the laughing **gas** that did me in. I tell you, the **grass** looked to be floating right up to the window that day. I had to **grasp** your grandma's arm just to keep steady. I wobbled out of that office like I was just learning to walk."

"But you know, those dentists get a bad **rap**," he continued. "That afternoon in the chair paid off. I haven't bought any candy in years," he said, taking a **sugar** cube from the front pocket of his overalls and popping it into his mouth.

Hannah S.

Sports mania

In honor of National Physical Fitness and Sports Month, see how quickly and accurately you can complete the items below.

1. List 20 different sports. _____
   _____
   _____
   _____

2. List 20 well-known athletes, 10 female and 10 male. _____
   _____
   _____
   _____

3. List 20 common terms used in sports. List the term and then the sport it is used in. (Example: *batting clean up: baseball*). _____
   _____
   _____
   _____

4. List 20 different well-known team names. (Example: *Detroit Lions)*_____
   _____
   _____
   _____

5. List 20 places where sports are commonly played. You may list general places, like "a baseball field," or specific places, like "Yankee Stadium." _____
   _____
   _____
   _____

6. List 20 things a person might have to do in a physical education class._____
   _____
   _____
   _____

7. Make up a sports category of your own and list 20 items that fit the category. _____
   _____
   _____
   _____

Answer key
Sports mania

Answers will vary. Here are some possibilities:

20 kinds of sports
1. football
2. basketball
3. tennis
4. volleyball
5. wrestling
6. skiing
7. ice skating
8. golf
9. swimming
10. bobsledding
11. bowling
12. karate
13. boxing
14. archery
15. fencing
16. gymnastics
17. hockey
18. soccer
19. speed skating
20. kayaking

20 well-known athletes
1. Cal Ripken
2. Deion Sanders
3. Pete Sampras
4. Jack Nicklaus
5. George Foreman
6. Michael Jordan
7. Mike Piazza
8. Greg Louganis
9. Andre Agassi
10. Wayne Gretsky
11. Oksana Baiul
12. Bonnie Blair
13. Jackie Joyner-Kersee
14. Amy Van Dyken
15. Shannon Miller
16. Monica Seles
17. Gabrielle Reece
18. Picabo Street
19. Nancy Lopez
20. Gabriella Sabatini

20 terms or phrases
1. love — tennis
2. Texas leaguer — baseball
3. first down — football
4. birdie — golf
5. spike — volleyball
6. point guard — basketball
7. dismount — gymnastics
8. triple axel — ice skating
9. conversions — soccer
10. power play — hockey
11. free throw — basketball
12. sacrifice bunt — baseball
13. slide tackle — soccer
14. laps — track
15. scrum — rugby
16. fastbreak — basketball
17. home run — baseball
18. bogey — golf
19. two-point conversion — football
20. hat trick — hockey

20 team names
1. Oakland Raiders
2. New York Yankees
3. Detroit Pistons
4. Los Angeles Kings
5. Duke Blue Devils
6. Colorado Rockies
7. Penn State Nitany Lions
8. Pittsburgh Steelers
9. Phoenix Suns
10. New York Rangers
11. Tampa Bay Buccaneers
12. Michigan Wolverines
13. Green Bay Packers
14. Boston Bruins
15. Colorado Avalanche
16. Tennessee Volunteers
17. St. Louis Cardinals
18. Detroit Tigers
19. Chicago Cubs
20. Texas Longhorns

20 places
1. Madison Square Garden
2. King Dome
3. Astro Dome
4. MGM Boxing Arena
5. LA Coliseum
6. Mile High Stadium
7. Wrigley Field
8. Belmont Park
9. Churchill Downs
10. Candlestick Park
11. Fenway Park
12. Wimbledon
13. Shea Stadium
14. Lambeau Field
15. Dodger Stadium
16. Rose Bowl
17. Spectrum in Philadelphia
18. McNichols Arena in Denver
19. Daytona International Speedway
20. Indianopolis Motor Speedway

20 things a person might have to do in a physical education class
1. jumping jacks
2. somersaults
3. push-ups
4. sit-ups
5. squat thrusts
6. chin-ups
7. toe touches
8. log rolls
9. pull-ups
10. play kick ball
11. play dodge ball
12. run laps
13. pick teams
14. jump rope
15. suit out
16. skip
17. play field hockey
18. weight lift
19. swim laps
20. climb the rope

20 sounds heard at a sporting event
1. crack of the bat
2. the swoosh of the basketball going through the net
3. the scrape of the ice with a hockey stick
4. cheering
5. whistle blowing
6. coaches yelling out plays
7. polite golf/tennis applause
8. the splash of water in swimming
9. bowling pins crashing down
10. football helmets cracking together
11. boos
12. vendors yelling things like "Get your hot dogs!"
13. the song "Take Me Out to the Ball Game"
14. feet stomping
15. horse hooves at the track
16. singing of the national anthem
17. the smack of a volleyball serve
18. the marching band at half-time
19. the music for a gymnastics floor routine
20. the announcer introducing players

Super shopper and the great whiner

Comic book heroes come with all kinds of special powers. Superman has X-ray vision, and Spiderman uses webs to scale walls. Wonder Woman spins faster than an ice skater while she changes clothes.

In honor of the anniversary of the publishing of the first comic book on May 3, 1934, create your own super hero. Give him or her whatever powers seem interesting to you. Super Shopper, for example, might zoom through the mall at the speed of light, finding the best bargains. The Great Whiner might manage to get his own way, in any situation. The Wizard of Gardening might make flowers bloom by just looking at them and shrivel weeds with only a glare.

Write a paragraph about your super hero, describing his or her powers.

_____

_____

_____

_____

_____

_____

_____

_____

_____

_____

_____

_____

_____

_____

Bonus

- Create a comic book cover, featuring your super hero.

OR

- Write the script for a comic book story featuring your super hero. Remember, a comic book tells a story almost entirely through pictures and dialogue.

Answer key
Super shopper and the great whiner

Answers will vary. Here is one possibility:

Stupendous Student uses osmosis to learn. She sleeps on her books and notes at night and remembers everything with her photographic memory. She gets perfect grades without even trying. At the same time, she is totally cool and has tons of friends. In fact, she often uses her powers to help other students who are having trouble in school. With just a touch of her hand, she can help someone figure out an algebra problem or remember when Lincoln gave the "Gettysburg Address." Here's a comic book cover featuring Stupendous Student:

Celestina T.

Mom's the word

Each sentence below contains the word *mother* in a different language. See if you can use the clues in each sentence (and an encyclopedia or atlas) to discover which language is used.

1. The favorite pastimes of my *mère* are visiting the Louvre and rowing on the Seine.
   Language _____

2. My *mutter* drives a Volkswagen and lives in Dresden.
   Language _____

3. My *anya* works in Budapest.
   Language _____

4. My *mat* can see St. Basil's Cathedral from the window of her flat.
   Language _____

5. My *mor* lives in Stockholm and loves films made by her countryman, Ingmar Bergman.
   Language _____

6. I love visiting my *madre* in Venice, where we travel down the Grand Canal.
   Language _____

7. Our Warsaw apartment smells so good when my *matka* cooks kielbasa.
   Language _____

8. My *aiti* keeps a copy of the *Kalevala* at her home in Helsinki.
   Language _____

9. I always eat sushi with my *haha* when we are on the island of Honshu.
   Language _____

10. My *anne* told me that Istanbul used to be called Constantinople.
    Language _____

11. One night at a luau with my *makuahine*, I thought I heard Mauna Loa erupting.
    Language _____

12. My *mãe* couldn't decide whether to take me to Rio de Janeiro or the the Amazon River.
    Language _____

13. When my *majka* and I visit Belgrade, we can see the Sava and Danube Rivers.
    Language _____

14. When my *moeder* and I went to Amsterdam, we visited the Van Gogh Museum.
    Language _____

15. I often hear my *ima* talk about when Golda Meir was prime minister.
    Language _____

Answer key
Mom's the word

1. French
2. German
3. Hungarian
4. Russian
5. Swedish
6. Italian
7. Polish
8. Finnish
9. Japanese
10. Turkish
11. Hawaiian
12. Portuguese
13. Serbian
14. Dutch
15. Hebrew

The Metropolitan Museum of YOU

International Museum Day — May 18

You have probably heard of the Metropolitan Museum of Art, the Guggenheim Museum, the Louvre or the Smithsonian Institute — all famous museums. In honor of International Museum Day, design a museum of your own, on the subject of YOU.

Design the museum to represent your personality. Do you like circles more than squares? Your museum might be spherical in shape. Is seven your favorite number? Your museum might be shaped like the number seven, or have seven floors, or have seven windows on each side. If you're a night owl, you might want your museum to be open from 10 p.m. to 6 a.m.

What would you put in your museum? What would help show who you are? A letter jacket? Your first bike? Your first *pointe* shoes? A slice of cake from your twelfth birthday party? Be creative. What kind of music would you play? Would you have hourly tours? Would you serve all your favorite foods in the cafeteria?

Describe your museum and draw a diagram of its floor plan.

Answers will vary. Here is one example:

To get to my museum you have to walk down a cobblestone path into an area surrounded by pine trees. The museum is in a large Victorian house with a lot of rooms, all decorated in lace curtains and ruffles. Each room has a bookcase. In one room I have my favorite children's books and my favorite dolls. I have a special doll that is about the size of a six-month-old baby. She wears real baby clothes. Around her are my favorite stuffed animals and the other dolls that I love. The book cases are filled with *Madeleine* books, Dr. Seuss books and all the books by Laura Ingalls Wilder.

Another room has my old ice skates, along with my favorite winter jacket that I had when I was ten, the one that made me feel great when I wore it. I have a table with all the pairs of glasses that I wore until I got contacts. In the closet of this room is the dress I wore to be in my cousin's wedding when I was six, the dress I got for my 12th birthday party and the outfit I wore on my first date.

The kitchen is an ice cream parlor. It serves only shakes, root beer floats, different kinds of ice cream cones and sundaes. People sit at a counter and take their time enjoying my favorite food. Sometimes I even drop by to enjoy it with them!

Mallory W.

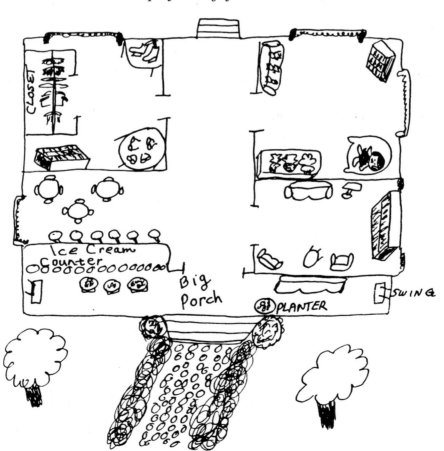

Off to join the circus

Circus Day — May 19

The circus has always fascinated people, young and old alike. It has an image of magic, excitement and glamour — a place where people perform amazing and impossible feats to cheers and whistles and endless rounds of applause.

Countless boys and girls fantasize about running away and joining the circus. Suppose that *you* were to become a circus performer. Who would you be? Would you become a trapeze artist, a sword swallower, a clown, a lion tamer, a juggler, the ringmaster, a tightrope walker, horseback rider or someone else? Why? How would you look and act? Describe yourself in your role as a circus performer.

Remember, you are writing about a fantasy world. In your fantasy world, you can be an acrobat, even if you can't turn a somersault in real life. Don't let reality hold you back!

_____

_____

_____

_____

_____

_____

_____

_____

_____

_____

_____

_____

_____

_____

_____

_____

_____

Bonus

Design the costume you would wear for your circus act. (Have as many sequins as you want!)

Answer key
Off to join the circus

Answers will vary. Here is one example:

If I were in the circus, I would be a tightrope walker. I'd have perfect balance and be very, very strong. I would be so strong, I could hold two women on my shoulders at the same time. (Of course, they would be beautiful women!) I would have a great body and be so handsome that all the girls and women watching me would dream about me. They would bribe the ticket takers to take flowers and notes to me.

I would perform amazing flips on the tightrope. I would ride a bicycle across it and walk on my hands across it and skip rope across it. I would be the most talented tightrope artist who ever lived, and "60 Minutes" would come and do a story about me.

I would love traveling all over the world with the circus. I would love being the best. I would love all the attention.

Here is the costume I would wear:

Chuck N.

Make your own memorial

Since the Civil War, the United States has celebrated Memorial Day (the last Monday of May), to honor American citizens killed in wars. Many people also look at the day as a day to honor any relatives and loved ones who have passed away.

One way to honor someone or something is by building monuments. If you took a stroll around Washington, D. C., you would see the Lincoln Memorial, the Jefferson Memorial and the Washington Monument, all commemorating former presidents. The National Vietnam Veterans Memorial is a monument to those who lost their lives in Vietnam. The United States Holocaust Memorial Museum recognizes the many victims of the holocaust of World War II.

Think of a person, a group or an event *you* think should not be forgotten. Then design a unique and appropriate monument to honor your subject.

You might choose someone living or dead, someone well-known or someone special only to you — a family member, a favorite teacher or even a pet. You might design a monument honoring a group of people, like working mothers or all the dogs you have ever owned. You might design a memorial for a certain event, like the founding of your town, the day your best friend was born or the day your brother's basketball team won the state championship.

Using your own paper, describe your monument and explain your choice of subjects. Be sure to include any symbolism or special features used in your design.

Bonus

Make a drawing of your design.

Answer key
Make your own memorial

Answers will vary. Here is one possibility:

In honor of the Bealer Sisters

The Bealer sisters live together in Milwaukee, Wisconsin, and they are two of the nicest people I have ever known. Anna is my grandma and Lydia is my great aunt. I think they need to have a monument to them because they are so cheerful and so nice and generous to their grandchildren. Whenever I go there I get so much attention and love, and I want them to know how much I appreciate them.

The monument would be a sculpture of a giant laughing mouth. It would represent all the laughter in their life. They tell jokes constantly, to each person who visits. They also laugh at their own jokes. They giggle together all the time and sound like young girls, even though they are both over 70.

The laughing mouth would have a drawer full of their best recipes, and anyone could take a copy. They both like to cook, and whenever someone visits, they make something homemade: chicken soup, pineapple cake, turkey dinners, rolls. It all tastes so good. Inside another drawer would be a deck of cards because they play cards all the time with their friends. Inside another drawer would be a baseball glove and bat for Grandma because she loves cheering for the Milwaukee Brewers and the Green Bay Packers. One more drawer would be full of books because Aunt Lydia loves to read.

On top of the bottom row of teeth, I would put pictures of all the people that Grandma and Aunt Lydia love: Grandma's children and grandchildren, Grandpa and all the friends that Aunt Lydia talks about all the time. The whole thing would be surrounded by thousands of tulips, daffodils, daisies, lilies of the valley, violets and pansies. These are all the pretty flowers that make me feel good, just the way these two people always make me feel.

Sophie K.

Bonus

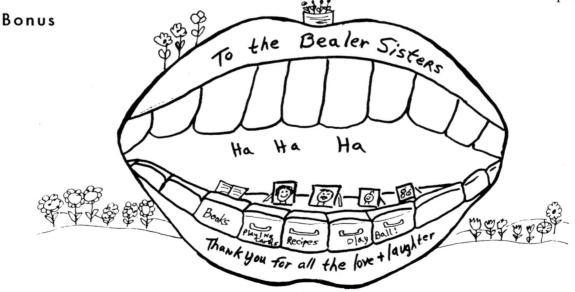

June

Lift every voice and sing

June is Black Music Month. In honor of black musical artists throughout history, complete the puzzle below. On the left is a list of some of the black artists who have made contributions to music and/or music history. On the right (and on the following pages) are facts about each particular artist. Using research and/or your own knowledge, find the name of the artist that matches each set of facts. An encyclopedia is a good place to start.

1. Richard Allen
2. Marian Anderson
3. Harry Belafonte
4. Chuck Berry
5. Thomas "Blind Tom" Greene Bethune
6. James Bland
7. James Brown
8. Nat "King" Cole
9. Bo Diddley
10. Ella Fitzgerald
11. LL Cool J
12. Herbie Hancock
13. Jimi Hendrix
14. Billie Holiday
15. Whitney Houston
16. Mahalia Jackson
17. Michael Jackson
18. Eva Jessye
19. Quincy Jones
20. Scott Joplin
21. Bob Marley
22. Wynton Marsalis
23. Leontyne Price
24. Bessie Smith
25. Stevie Wonder

A)_____

- born Eleanora Fagan, but adopted her name from her favorite movie star
- nicknamed "Lady Day"
- wrote autobiography *Lady Sings the Blues*
- known for recording "Strange Fruit" and "Driving Me Crazy"

B)_____

- grew up in an orphanage in Yonkers, New York
- known around the world as "the First Lady of Song"
- recorded "A-Tisket, A-Tasket" with Chick Webb in 1935

C)_____

- sold more than two million copies of "Down Hearted Blues"
- known as the "Empress of Jazz"
- made a short motion picture, *St. Louis Blues* in 1929

D)_____

- awarded Medal of Freedom from Lyndon Johnson in 1963
- known by many as the world's greatest concert contralto
- first African-American singer to perform as a member of the Metropolitan Opera in New York City

E)_____

- Born in Rhoden Hall, St. Ann, Jamaica
- First group, the Rudeboys, eventually became the Wailers
- Was shot and wounded while giving a free concert in Kingston

F)_____

- refused to sing anything but religious songs
- never sang anywhere liquor was served
- sang at the inauguration of President John F. Kennedy
- first great hit was "Move on Up a Little Higher"

G)_____

- Owned recording studios, three radio stations and a real estate company
- Appeared in the film *The Blues Brothers*
- Considered the "Godfather of Soul"

H)_____

- Moved to Jamaica with his mother when he was a child
- First great success was the album *Calypso*, which included the hit "Banana Boat Song" (popularly known as "Day-O") in 1956
- First black man to win an Emmy award
- UNICEF Goodwill Ambassador and winner of Peace Corps award Leader of Peace

I)_____

- Born Ellas Bates McDaniel, his stage name was slang for "mischievous child"
- Flamboyant performer known for playing square, fur-covered guitars
- Appeared in Nike ads with Bo Jackson

J)_____

- First hit, "Maybellene" was one of the first songs to become number one on three different charts: pop, rhythm and blues and country western
- Famous for legendary "duck walk" dance step, a combination of crouching, walking and playing guitar
- Performed rock classics such as "Rock 'n' Roll Music" and "Johnny B. Goode"

K)_____

- Jazz pianist of the 1940s
- Recording of Mel Torme's "The Christmas Song" was a hit in 1946
- Song "Mona Lisa" won an Academy Award in 1950 as the theme song for the movie *Captain Carey, U.S.A.*
- His daughter redid his hit "Unforgettable"

L)_____

- Pioneer of the jazz-fusion style
- Performed a Mozart piano concerto with the Chicago Symphony Orchestra at the age of 11
- Discovered "scratch" music, a rhythmic effect often used in early rap music
- Received an Academy Award in 1986 for the score of the movie *Round Midnight*

M)_____

- Known for "Wild Thing," "Purple Haze" and "The Wind Cries Mary"
- Performed legendary version of "The Star Spangled Banner" in which he plucked the guitar with his teeth
- Died of drug overdose

N)_____

- First performer to have seven consecu- tive number one singles on pop music charts
- Sang backup for Chaka Khan and Lou Rawls
- Starred in movies *The Bodyguard* and *Waiting to Exhale.*

O)_____

- Played the Scarecrow in the musical film *The Wiz*
- Album *Thriller* earned an unprece- dented eight Grammy Awards
- With Lionel Richie, wrote the song "We Are the World," donating profits to al- leviate world hunger

P)_____

- In 1984, became the first musician to win Grammy Awards in both jazz and classical music in the same year
- In 1993, released "Citi Movement," a score for modern ballet which combined classical and jazz music
- Artistic director for the "Jazz at Lincoln Center" program in New York City

Q)_____

- Born a slave in Philadelphia in 1760
- Organizer of the first congregation of the African Methodist Episcopalian (AME) Church
- Published in 1801 *A Collection of Spiri- tual Songs and Hymns Selected from Vari- ous Authors*, the first hymnal designed exclusively for an all-black congrega- tion
- In 1816 was elected the first black bishop in the United States

R)_____

- First success on Motown label at age 13
- Blind since infancy, began playing piano at age 4
- Hits include, "You Are the Sunshine of My Life" and "Superstition"

S)_____

- Known as the "voice of the century" and the "girl with the golden voice"
- Her performance of Lenora in Verdi's *Il Trovatore* at her debut in 1961 received a 42-minute ovation from the audience at the Metropolitan Opera House
- Received the Italian Award of Merit for her contributions to Italian music
- First African-American to star in an op- era on television

T)_____

- Considered "King of Ragtime"
- Wrote "The Entertainer"
- His *Maple Leaf Rag*, titled after the Maple Leaf Club where he worked, sold hundreds of thousands of copies in the first decade of its publicaton
- Wrote the opera, *Treemonisha* in 1911

U)_____

- Considered "The World's Greatest Minstrel Man" and "The Idol of the Music Halls"
- Wrote approximately 700 songs, includ- ing "In the Evening by the Moonlight" and "Oh, Dem Golden Slippers"
- When 24 years old, published "Carry Me Back to Old Virginny" which (62 years later) became the official state song of Virginia
- Taught himself the banjo

V)_____

- The first African-American woman to win international distinction as the director of a professional choral group
- Served as choral director for Gershwin's first production of *Porgy and Bess* in 1935
- Published *Paradise Lost and Regained,* music arranged around John Milton's work by the same name

W)_____

- Slave whose owner's family made a fortune off his musical ability
- Known for his musical memory, he could play any song he listened to and never forgot a piece once he learned it
- Despite no musical training, could play as many as seven hundred piano pieces upon demand
- At the White House, played correctly a 20-page piece shortly after hearing it

X)_____

- Co-produced the movie *The Color Purple*
- Appointed vice-president of Mercury Records in 1964
- Helped produce *We Are the World*
- Won 26 Grammy Awards
- Produced Michael Jackson's album *Thriller*

Y)_____

- Born James Todd Smith, he was rapping by the time he was 9
- Has earned five multi-platinum albums and a Grammy Award
- Performed at the Inaugural ceremony celebration for President Clinton
- Works with a number of charitable organizations and founded a summer camp that stresses cultural awareness through educational guidance and sports

Bonus

Choose one of the following activities:

- Do more research on one of the artists above. Write about the life and musical contributions of the artist.

- Pick a song written, played or sung by any of the above artists and write a review of it.

- Find five black musicians who are not on the above list. Explain briefly why they should be included on the list, and write down five facts about each one of them.

Answer key
Lift every voice and sing

A) Billie Holiday
B) Ella Fitzgerald
C) Bessie Smith
D) Marian Anderson
E) Bob Marley
F) Mahalia Jackson
G) James Brown
H) Harry Belafonte
I) Bo Diddley
J) Chuck Berry
K) Nat "King" Cole
L) Herbie Hancock
M) Jimi Hendrix
N) Whitney Houston
O) Michael Jackson
P) Wynton Marsalis
Q) Richard Allen
R) Stevie Wonder
S) Leontyne Price
T) Scott Joplin
U) James Bland
V) Eva Jessye
W) Thomas "Blind Tom" Greene Bethune
X) Quincy Jones
Y) LL Cool J

Stupid pet tricks

In honor of National Adopt a Cat Month, imagine that you adopt a cat — or any other animal — from your local animal shelter. You get your pet home and you find that it has an amazing ability. Perhaps you discover that your cat juggles or that your boa constrictor sings opera or that your hamster tap dances.

Your pet is so amazing that you decide to try to get him or her on the "Stupid Pet Tricks" feature of the *Late Show with David Letterman.* (In case you have never seen it, this segment of the show features real people and their talented pets, who always perform very unusual tricks.)

Write Letterman a letter, persuading him that your pet is worthy of appearing on television. In your letter be sure to address the following:

- What kind of animal is your pet?
- What is his or her name? Is there any special significance to the name? If so, what?
- What is your pet's amazing talent? Describe it in detail.
- Why should your pet appear on the *Late Show with David Letterman?*
- Is there any other information that Letterman should have about your pet? If so, what is it?

Answer key
Stupid pet tricks

Answers will vary. Here is one example:

Dear Mr. David Letterman:

Please consider my Chihuahua Frankie as a candidate for "Stupid Pet Tricks." Frankie is an accordion-playing Chihuahua, named after the polka king Frankie Yankovic.

Frankie has a certain star quality in both his looks and his personality. Even though he shakes a lot, I think his sleek brown body and twinkling eyes are hard to resist. He works very hard to learn the fast and cheerful polkas that he plays.

Frankie has been playing an accordion since he was only a puppy. He stands on his hind legs, puts his paws on the keyboard and buttons, and squeezes out traditional folk music. Of course he uses a tiny toy accordion.

Mr. Letterman, I think you will agree that an accordion-playing Chihuahua is a pretty incredible little animal. Please, consider having Frankie on your show.

Sincerely,

Carmen Petrovich
Frankie's owner

Foot cheese and other family phrases

June 13 is Family History Day. Instead of diagramming your family tree, try digging around at its roots. Look at what makes your family special. One thing that makes a family special is its history, including all the special words, phrases, names, jokes and habits that tie a family together.

Special words and phrases. Family members tend to develop special words and phrases that are unique to them. For example, everyone in one family calls parmesan cheese "foot cheese." (At some point, a child in the family took a whiff of some parmesan and said, "Yuk! This stuff smells like stinky feet!" From that moment on, it's been "Pass the foot cheese.")

Inside jokes. Most families have inside jokes. For example, at every holiday gathering in one family, someone says, "And you prepare the ginger root." Everyone cracks up, every time, and no one understands the joke except family members. Visitors just scratch their heads and wonder, "What's so funny about ginger root?"

Special names. A mother in one family calls her daughter "Bird," even though her name is "Rani." A grandfather calls his son "Hoss" and his grandson "Hossley," but their names are Peter and Joshua. Family members have forgotten where the names came from, if they ever even knew. They just accept them as part of the family tradition.

Mystery terms. Sometimes family phrases make no sense at all, even to family members themselves. For example, one girl grew up hearing people refer to getting married as "going to the sweet shop." She finally asked why family members used the phrase, and someone eventually remembered that her grandparents had been married in a bakery called the Sweet Shop.

Family habits. Habits of some family members often embarrass, annoy or amuse other family members. It's a family tradition to laugh at or complain about these habits. For example, everyone in one family cringes, looks down, and tries not to giggle whenever they go out to eat and a waiter asks, "Would you like dessert?" That's because they know, absolutely KNOW, that Grandma will tell the waiter the whole story of how she would *like* to have dessert but she has this digestive condition, and sugar's not good for her, so even though she likes dessert very much, she really shouldn't have it, although a bite or two of someone else's dessert wouldn't hurt her, if others would like to have dessert. And, no, she can't have coffee either. She likes coffee, but coffee just doesn't like *her*, and, no, it doesn't matter if it's decaffeinated because the chemicals they use to decaffeinate coffee are actually worse for you than the caffeine itself.

In honor of Family History Day, think about *your* special family names and phrases. Think about family stories, inside jokes, nicknames and traditions. Choose one or more stories to write about and share. (Since friends are often as close as family, you might instead want to write about a special story, name, joke, language or tradition you share with your friends.)

Answer key
Foot cheese and other family phrases

Answers will vary. Here is one possibility:

One year when my brother and sister and I were small, we had a horrible hail storm that caused lots of damage in our community. It seemed like all the adults ever talked about was hail damage.

Shortly after that, we were in the car driving to see my grandma, who lived an hour away. We saw a house that was so old that the roof had completely caved in. I yelled, "Hail damage!" Since it obviously wasn't hail damage, my parents just started laughing. After that, we started seeing who could find the most "hail damages." About 30 miles out of town, we came across the ultimate "hail damage." It was an old, old house that had only a floor and 1 1/2 walls left. We all agreed that that house should win the award for the most hail damage.

From that day forward, any time we drove by that house, we competed to see who could call "ultimate hail damage" first. It was all-out competition. We tried to distract the others so we could call it first. Or we would pinch the others so that they would be in too much pain to call it. The prize was great: whoever called the ultimate hail damage first immediately became Ruler of the World — at least until the next time we passed the house.

Jack B.

It's a grand old flag

"Every heart beats true for the red, white and blue . . . . ." is a line from the song "It's a Grand Old Flag," written by composer George M. Cohan. The song is a perfect one for Flag Day, June 14.

In honor of Flag Day, take a look at the flag facts and flag etiquette, below.

Flag facts

- The Second Continental Congress of Philadelphia adopted the design for the first U.S. flag on June 14, 1777.
- The 13 stars in the original flag represented the 13 united colonies.
- The white stars on a blue field represent a new constellation.
- Some flag characteristics are universal. A white flag indicates a surrender. A yellow flag is the sign of the presence of an infectious disease. A nation shows mourning by flying its flags at half-mast.

Flag etiquette

- The flag should not be displayed during bad weather, unless the flag is made of all-weather material.
- It should not be displayed before sunrise or after sunset, unless it is illuminated.
- It should not be placed under any other flag.
- Displaying the flag with the stars down is a sign of extreme danger to life or property.
- Those raising the flag should do so briskly and lower it ceremoniously.

Try designing a flag yourself. You might design a flag for your school, for your town, for a club or organization, for your family or even for yourself. Plan your flag with great care, just as the designers of the original Stars and Stripes thought carefully about the meaning of the colors and design they chose.

- Draw your flag, or make a model of it.
- Describe the meaning of the design.
- Make a list of flag etiquette "dos and don'ts" for your flag.

Answer key
It's a grand old flag

Answers will vary. Here is one possibility:

The background to my flag represents my dreams and goals. I made it look like the sky because I believe "The sky is the limit."

I chose a circle for my flag to show that I am a fairly well-rounded person. I like many, many activities, from basketball and dancing to reading and playing chess. There is a part of a sun in the circle, and also part of a moon. I put the sun in because I am a happy person who loves to laugh. Also, I really love sunshine and everything that comes with it, like summertime. I put the moon in to show the other side of my personality, which is thoughtful and quiet. The edge of the circle is colored purple because, to me, purple represents creativity. I think I am a very creative person. Also, the flag should be made out of silk, just because I love silk!

Flag etiquette: People should respect my flag as much as they respect me. My flag should hang somewhere in my house on my birthday.

Carmen D.

Juggle those "ug" words

When you look through a dictionary, you won't find all that many words with the sound "ug" in them. "Juggle" is one of them.

In honor of National Juggling Day, think of "ug" words. See if you can translate each description below into a two-word phrase, with *both* words having the "ug" sound. (Hint: Use a thesaurus and a dictionary for help.)

Example:

Cardboard suitcases:
corrugated luggage

1. Athletic little watercraft: _____

2. Grunt uttered by a thief: _____

3. Self-satisfied circus entertainer: _____

4. Fight between two small dogs with snub noses: _____

5. Cozy insect: _____

6. Cuddly pharmacist: _____

7. Baseball player's hangout: _____

8. Extremely slow embrace: _____

9. Very unattractive hunk of gold: _____

10. Slimy creature's carpet: _____

11. Ruffian gulping a drink: _____

12. Over-medicated illegal exporter: _____

Bonus

See if you can add at least two items of your own to the puzzle above. Each description you write should have a two-word answer, with both words containing "ug."

Then see if you can write a description with a *three* word answer, with all three words containing "ug."

Answer key
Juggle those "ug" words

1. rugged tugboat
2. mugger's ugh
3. smug juggler
4. pug struggle
5. snug bug
6. snuggling druggist
7. slugger's dugout
8. sluggish hug
9. ugly nugget
10. slug's rug
11. chugging thug
12. drugged smuggler

Bonus

Answers will vary. Here are some possibilities:

Two carriages fighting over one blanket: buggy tug-of-war
The yank of an electrical outlet: plug tug
Homely drinking container for a rough sport: ugly rugby mug

For the birds

Congress chose the bald eagle as our national symbol in 1782, although Ben Franklin is said to have coyly suggested the turkey, instead.

When people think of a bald eagle, words like *honor*, *grandeur* and *freedom* usually come to mind. What comes to mind when you think of other birds? On the left, below, is a list of birds. On the right is a list of words commonly associated with these birds. Match each bird with the correct words on the right.

_____ 1. stork	A. grace, ballets, weddings
_____ 2. penguin	B. coward
_____ 3. canary	C. rising out of the ashes
_____ 4. raven	D. head in the sand
_____ 5. chicken	E. NBC
_____ 6. goose	F. tuxedos
_____ 7. peacock	G. crazy as a
_____ 8. lark	H. Polly want a cracker
_____ 9. ostrich	I. spring
_____ 10. dove	J. tacky lawn ornaments
_____ 11. vulture	K. happy as a
_____ 12. pink flamingos	L. babies
_____ 13. swans	M. peace
_____ 14. parrot	N. Edgar Allen Poe
_____ 15. phoenix	O. silly
_____ 16. blue bird	P. Tweety Bird
_____ 17. loon	Q. happiness
_____ 18. jay bird	R. cock-a-doodle-doo
_____ 19. sparrow	S. naked as a
_____ 20. robin	T. eats like a
_____ 21. duck	U. waddles like a
_____ 22. crow	V. "Beep beep"
_____ 23. roadrunner	W. scavenger, death
_____ 24. hawk	X. boast
_____ 25. rooster	Y. watch like a

Bonus

Now see if you can add three more items to the puzzle above.

Answer key
For the birds

1. L
2. F
3. P
4. N
5. B
6. O
7. E
8. K
9. D
10. M
11. W
12. J
13. A
14. H
15. C
16. Q
17. G
18. S
19. T
20. I
21. U
22. X
23. V
24. Y
25. R

Bonus

1. owl — wise
2. cuckoo — gives you the time of day
3. toucan — Fruit Loops mascot

Advice for moms and dads

In honor of Father's Day, think about what advice *you* would give future fathers (and mothers, too). What are 12 things a parent should NEVER do? What are 12 things a parent absolutely SHOULD do, in your opinion?

Parents should NEVER:

1. _____
_____

2. _____
_____

3. _____
_____

4. _____
_____

5. _____
_____

6. _____
_____

7. _____
_____

8. _____
_____

9. _____
_____

10. _____
_____

11. _____
_____

12. _____
_____

Parents SHOULD:

1. _____
_____

2. _____
_____

3. _____
_____

4. _____
_____

5. _____
_____

6. _____
_____

7. _____
_____

8. _____
_____

9. _____
_____

10. _____
_____

11. _____
_____

12. _____
_____

Answer key
Advice for moms and dads

Answers will vary. Here are some possibilities:

Parents should NEVER:

1. talk about how *easy* their kids have it.
2. tell their kids to get off the phone unless someone is expecting a very, very important call.
3. make their kids eat everything on their plate.
4. lecture their kids about responsibility.
5. pressure their kids about grades and school.
6. nag.
7. ignore their kids.
8. invade their child's privacy.
9. give their child a lecture in front of people who aren't family members.
10. tease their kids about the opposite sex.
11. say, "Because I said so."
12. complain about MTV.

Parents SHOULD:

1. ignore the mess in a teenager's room, unless it's health-threatening.
2. ground their kids when they misbehave.
3. let their kids dress however they want.
4. have their kids help cook dinner and wash the dishes.
5. give their kids an allowance.
6. play with their kids a lot.
7. encourage their children to try anything they want to try, as long it won't hurt them
8. listen.
9. let their kids stay up as late as they want sometimes.
10. let their kids date who they want.
11. attend all their child's concerts, games, performances, etc.
12. say, "Good job" whenever it is appropriate.

Letting go

You have probably heard of the Hatfields and the McCoys, two legendary families who nurtured a grudge against each other for generations. Their grudge often resulted in violence.

Not all grudges end in violence, but all grudges *do* cause damage. Unfortunately, much of the damage is often to the person holding the grudge. For example, suppose that a child is furious with her mother and refuses to get over it. When something wonderful happens to her, she may not feel she can share her great news with her mother, as she normally would. She doesn't get to hear her mother's warm praise or feel her hug or enjoy going out to dinner to celebrate.

The fourth Sunday in June is National Forgiveness Day, designed to give people everywhere an excuse to let go of grudges, to forgive others for not being perfect and to go on with their lives. In recognition of National Forgiveness Day, take out a piece of paper and write about a grudge you are currently holding against someone. Who is it that you are mad at or annoyed with? Why? For your eyes only, write about what happened. Get all your anger out on paper.

Then resolve to let go of your grudge. Fold up your paper, tear it apart and throw it away, putting an end to your grudge forever.

July

Television title search

What is the first thing many people do when they are bored? They turn on the television. If they are really bored, it doesn't matter what's on. They will watch just about anything.

In honor of National Anti-Boredom Month, try doing something *instead* of watching television. Use all your television knowledge to complete the puzzle below. You may use titles of old or new television shows. Give yourself one point for each correct answer to the puzzle below. An average score is two correct answers for each item. Use your own paper.

Name at least one television show that:

1. Has a female name in the title
2. Has a grandfather in the cast
3. Has a title that is a complete sentence
4. Is set in an office
5. Stars a bald person
6. Has a verb in the title
7. Has a title made up of only one noun and no other words
8. Has an adjective in the title
9. Stars an actor with a mustache
10. Is set in a southern city
11. Is set in New York City
12. Has a conjunction in the title
13. Has the word "love" in the title
14. Has a preposition in the title
15. Features cartoon animals
16. Features a person or an animal with magical or supernatural powers
17. Has an abbreviation in the title
18. Includes an alien from another planet in the cast
19. Is set in a West Coast city
20. Has numbers in the title

Bonus

Now add 5 items of your own to the puzzle above. Be sure to include an answer key.

Answers will vary. Here are some possibilities:

		Score
1.	Roseanne. Ellen.	2
2.	My Three Sons. The Waltons. The Simpsons.	3
3.	I Love Lucy. Life Goes On. Get Smart.	3
4.	Murphy Brown. Mary Tyler Moore Show.	2
5.	Frasier. All in the Family.	2
6.	Get Smart. Leave it to Beaver.	2
7.	Taxi. Friends. Wings.	3
8.	Happy Days. Green Acres.	2
9.	Dukes of Hazzard. The Addams Family.	2
10.	Designing Women. Dallas.	2
11.	Mad About You. The Jeffersons. Seinfeld.	3
12.	Lois and Clark. The Young and the Restless.	2
13.	Love Boat. I Love Lucy.	2
14.	Grace Under Fire. Days of Our Lives. One Life to Live.	3
15.	Ren and Stimpy. Looney Toons.	2
16.	I Dream of Jeannie. Bewitched.	2
17.	M.A.S.H. E.R.	2
18.	Alf. Third Rock from the Sun.	2
19.	L.A. Law. Beverly Hillbillies. Frasier.	3
20.	Three's Company. 60 Minutes. 20/20. Beverly Hills 90210.	4
	Total	48

Bonus

Answers will vary. Here are some possibilities:

1. Is set in a school: Head of the Class. Saved by the Bell.
2. Is set in a hospital: E.R. Chicago Hope. General Hospital.
3. Stars an animal: Flipper. Lassie.
4. Has the word "family" in the title: Family Ties. Family Matters.
5. Takes place in a small rural town: The Waltons. Green Acres.

We all scream for ice cream

In honor of National Ice Cream Month, see if your group can think of a flavor, brand-name or type of ice cream that begins with each letter of the alphabet. If you can think of more than one answer that begins with a certain letter, choose the answer that you think the other groups might *not* choose. (Note: You must use generally known flavors, brand names and types of ice cream treats. Yes, someone somewhere has probably made dill pickle ice cream. However, it's not a generally known flavor, so it won't count here.) Your group will receive one point for each correct answer, unless no other group has that answer. Then you will receive 3 points for that answer. If you aren't able to come up with an answer for an item, *subtract* one point for that item.

List your points to the left of each letter.

_____ A. _____	_____ N. _____
_____ B. _____	_____ O. _____
_____ C. _____	_____ P. _____
_____ D. _____	_____ Q. _____
_____ E. _____	_____ R. _____
_____ F. _____	_____ S. _____
_____ G. _____	_____ T. _____
_____ H. _____	_____ U. _____
_____ I. _____	_____ V. _____
_____ J. _____	_____ W. _____
_____ K. _____	_____ X. _____
_____ L. _____	_____ Y. _____
_____ M. _____	_____ Z. _____
_____ Score (subtotal)	_____ Score (subtotal)

_____ Total score

Answers will vary, and there may not be an answer for every letter. Here are some possible answers:

Score	Ice cream
1	A. almond nut crunch
2	B. butter brickle, butterscotch
1	C. chocolate chip cookie dough
3	D. Dreyer's
1	E. egg nog
1	F. fudge ripple
1	G. German chocolate cake
1	H. hazelnut
1	I. Irish creme
1	J. jamoca almond fudge
1	K. Klondike Bars
1	L. lemon
1	M. marshmallow swirl
1	N. neopolitan
1	O. orange cream
2	P. peach, Pralines 'N Cream
-1	Q. —
1	R. rocky road
1	S. strawberry
1	T. tin roof sundae
-1	U. —
1	V. vanilla
1	W. Wavy Gravy
1	X. Xtra Berrylicious
-1	Y. —
-1	Z. —
22	Total

Stamp out boring stamps

On July 1, 1847, the United States Post Office issued its first official adhesive postage stamp. Since then, stamps have been designed to commemorate every subject imaginable, from Elvis Presley to the space program to endangered species of animals.

Some postage stamps have been, well, a bit boring. For example, think about the U.S. flag stamp we see year after year. It's white, and a flag is stuck in the middle. There's no "pizzazz" to the design.

What if we could all design our own personal stamps and have them printed? If you love tropical fish, you might design a beautiful turquoise, gold and orange fish stamp. If you love skateboarding or playing pool, you might design a skateboarding stamp or a pool stamp. Maybe you would like to design a stamp made up of just your favorite colors or a stamp honoring your favorite television show or musical group.

Go ahead and design an interesting stamp that you — and maybe others, too — would like to use. Remember, your design must be fairly simple and clear because you don't have much space. Put a copy of your design in the space below. To the right, describe why you have chosen the design. What is its meaning to you? Why did you choose the colors and shapes you have chosen?

Answer key
Stamp out boring stamps

Answers will vary. Here is one example:

I designed a stamp in honor of redheads because I have red hair. I made the hair the main feature of the stamp, for obvious reasons. I used the words "1 out of 40" on the stamp because only one out of 40 people is a redhead. I used a yellow background so that the red would stand out even more clearly.

Kylie J.

Four for the Fourth

In honor of America's birthday, Independence Day, see if you can complete the special American history quiz below. Because Independence Day is always celebrated on July 4th, every answer to the quiz includes at least one word that is 4 letters long.

Example

He said, "I only regret that I have but one life to live for my country."
*Nathan **Hale***

1. She sewed the first flying "symbol" of our country:

    __ __ __ __ __   __ __ __ __ __

2. Slain leader of the civil rights movement:

    __ __ __ __ __ __ __   __ __ __ __ __ __ __ __   __ __ __ __ __, __ __

3. It sailed the ocean blue in 1492: __ __ __ __

4. First "inalienable right" stated in the Declaration of Independence: __ __ __ __

5. Famous midnight rider: __ __ __ __   __ __ __ __ __ __

6. First 10 amendments to the Constitution:

    __ __ __ __   __ __ __   __ __ __ __ __ __ __

7. Reason why people moved to California in the 1800s: __ __ __ __

8. Horace Greeley said young men should go to this part of the country: __ __ __ __

9. Mail delivery system in the 1800s: __ __ __ __   __ __ __ __ __ __ __

10. Thomas Jefferson's first vice-president: __ __ __ __ __ __   __ __ __ __

11. He developed the first assembly line to manufacture automobiles:

    __ __ __ __ __ __   __ __ __ __

12. Man whose name was used in a famous Supreme Court decision on slavery:

    __ __ __ __ __   __ __ __ __ __ __

13. Waterway in New York state made famous in folk song:

    __ __ __ __ __   __ __ __ __ __

14. Where the United States stores money: ___ ___ ___ ___   ___ ___ ___ ___

15. Situation between Communist U.S.S.R. and the US after WWII:

    ___ ___ ___ ___   ___ ___ ___

16. Failed invasion by U.S. forces in 1961: ___ ___ ___   ___ ___   ___ ___ ___ ___ ___

17. Country where the invasion of #16 took place: ___ ___ ___ ___ ___

18. What President Franklin Roosevelt promised the country in 1932:

    ___ ___ ___   ___ ___ ___ ___

19. Anthem written by Francis Scott Key:

    ___ ___ ___ ___   ___ ___ ___ ___ ___ ___ ___ ___   ___ ___ ___ ___ ___

20. He killed assassin Lee Harvey Oswald in 1963: ___ ___ ___ ___   ___ ___ ___ ___

21. First American woman to ride in space: ___ ___ ___ ___ ___   ___ ___ ___ ___

22. Where the Great Crash of 1929 occurred: ___ ___ ___ ___   ___ ___ ___ ___ ___ ___

23. Nickname for the first trains: ___ ___ ___ ___   ___ ___ ___ ___ ___

24. What the United States celebrates on June 14: ___ ___ ___ ___   ___ ___ ___

25. Abbreviation for America's space agency: ___ ___ ___ ___

Bonus

1. Add four more questions about American history to this quiz. Remember: Every answer should contain at least one word with four letters.

2. Name the four U.S. Presidents who each had a four-letter last name.

3. Name the three states that have four-letter names.

4. List four American cities that have four-letter names.

Answer key
Four for the Fourth

1. Betsy Ross
2. Martin Luther King, Jr.
3. Nina
4. "Life"
5. Paul Revere
6. Bill of Rights
7. Gold
8. West
9. Pony Express
10. Aaron Burr
11. Henry Ford
12. Dred Scott
13. Erie Canal
14. Fort Knox
15. Cold War
16. Bay of Pigs
17. Cuba
18. New Deal
19. Star Spangled Banner
20. Jack Ruby
21. Sally Ride
22. Wall Street
23. Iron horses
24. Flag Day
25. NASA

Bonus

1. Answers will vary. Some possibilities: What showman was known for his "Wild West Show"? (Buffalo Bill Cody) Who was the first man to walk on the moon? (Neil Armstrong) What woman is famous for not giving up her seat on a bus? (Rosa Parks) Who invented the sewing machine? (Elias Howe)
2. James K. Polk, William Taft, Gerald Ford, George Bush
3. Iowa, Ohio, Utah
4. Answers will vary. Some possibilities: Moab, Utah. Taos, New Mexico. Reno, Nevada. Waco, Texas.

Math under the big top

P.T. Barnum, one of the creators of the Barnum and Bailey Circus, is often called "the greatest showman who ever lived." In 1919 he combined his circus with the circus started by the seven Ringling brothers, forming the Ringling Brothers and Barnum & Bailey Circus.

Below are some interesting statistics about the Ringling Brothers and Barnum & Bailey Circus*:

- Each year, the Ringling Brothers and Barnum & Bailey Circus entertains 25 million people in 97 countries.

- It uses more than 1000 costumes.

- It takes about 8 hours to set up before each performance.

- Each year circus workers feed their animals 364 tons of hay; 46,800 lbs. of meat; 62,400 lbs. of carrots; 39,000 lbs. of apples and 15,288 loaves of bread.

- The circus animals include 42 elephants, 10 lions, 14 tigers, 6 bears, 33 horses, 2 camels, 2 llamas and 4 zebras.

- Each year the circus puts on approximately 1075 performances.

- When the circus train of 53 cars is fully loaded, it weighs one and a half billion lbs.

---

*The statistics are from *The Book of Lists for Kids* (Houghton Mifflin Company, 1995), by Sandra and Harry Choron.

Use the statistics above to answer the following questions:

1. How many striped animals does the circus have? _____

2. How many ounces of apples does the circus use each year? _____

3. If the circus buys carrots in 3-pound bags, how many bags of carrots do they need each year? _____

4. If the whole circus train weighs 1.5 billion lbs., how much would the average individual car weigh, if each car weighed the same amount? _____

5. How many *pounds* of hay does the circus use each year? _____

The questions above were just for warm-up. Now use the same statistics to solve the problem below.

The Lion's Share

Lola the Lion Feeder was just hired by the Ringling Brothers and Barnum & Bailey Circus, and she desperately needs your help. When Robby Ringleader hired her, he stressed the importance of feeding the lions the same amount of meat every day. He said, "Any more or any less food and you might just become their dessert." At first Lola shrugged off his warnings, thinking, "It can't be that important." Then she started noticing that the lions were eyeing her very carefully, and she got nervous. She decided she had better figure out exactly how much meat to give the lions each day.

Robby Ringleader gave her the following information to use in figuring out how much to feed each lion:

- Out of the total pounds of meat the circus uses each year, the lions receive 34 percent.
- Out of the total amount of meat that all the lions receive each **day**, each individual lion receives the percent of food shown below.

Leo, 15%	Lisa, 9%
Linda, 8%	Lilly, 6%
Lyle, 7%	Ludwig, 18%
Luke, 11%	Laura, 10%
Luther, 12%	Lolita, 4%

What is the exact amount of meat that each lion should get each day?

(This problem can be tricky. Here is a hint: Remember that after you figure how much meat the lions eat each year, you need to figure how much they eat each day. Also, it is okay to round the nearest whole number.)

Bonus

This is for the extra brave. Create your own story problem based on the statistics about the Ringling Brothers and Barnum & Bailey Circus. Remember to make an answer key for your problem.

1. 18 striped animals
2. 624,000 ounces
3. 20,800 3-lb. bags
4. 28,301,886.75 lbs.
5. 728,000 lbs.

Out of the total pounds of meat each year, the lions receive 34%, or 15,912 lbs. That is 43.59 lbs. each day for all the lions. Each individual lion receives the percent of food shown below (answers rounded to the nearest hundredth):

Leo, 15% or 6.54 lbs.

Linda, 8%, or 3.49 lbs.

Lyle, 7%, or 3.05 lbs.

Luke, 11%, or 4.79 lbs.

Luther, 12%, or 5.23 lbs.

Lisa, 9%, or 3.92 lbs.

Lilly, 6%, or 2.62 lbs.

Ludwig, 18%, or 7.85 lbs.

Laura, 10%, or 4.36 lbs.

Lolita, 4%, or 1.74 lbs.

Bonus

Answers will vary. Here is one possibility:

Bonita Bellini, the bearded lady, was sent to the store to buy carrots for the animals for the month of March. If she could buy the carrots only in 5 lb. bags, how many bags would she need to buy just for the month of March? If the bags cost her $2.34 each, how much would all the carrots cost?

(She would need 5200 lbs. of carrots, or 1040 bags. The cost would be $2433.60.)

Alex T.

Clapping for the clerihew

July 10 marks the birthday of Edmund Clerihew Bentley, the inventor of the clerihew.

If you are like most people, you have never heard of Bentley and have no idea what in the world a clerihew is. Well, it's time that you are enlightened!

A clerihew is a four-line humorous poem made up of two rhyming couplets. (A rhyming couplet, in case you aren't familiar with the term, is simply two lines that rhyme.) In a clerihew, a person's name is usually mentioned in the first line of the first couplet. Each line of the couplet is usually of unequal length, and the words don't have to rhyme all that well. In fact, sometimes the poem is more amusing when the rhyme is awkward or the words just *sort of* rhyme.

Examples

> The love of Josh and Kate
> is great.
> They think that their future will be heaven.
> They're seven.

> I work with a guy named Alexander
> who told me with great candor
> that if we let our computers catch a virus
> our boss will fire us.

In honor of Clerihew Day, write a clerihew about yourself, a friend, a family member or a pet. Use a name in the first line. Remember that the poem must have four lines with two rhyming couplets that are not the same length. Even though the poem must be humorous, remember to be nice.

Bonus

Now that you have the idea of the clerihew down, see if you can write three clerihews that are all related in some way. The clerihews might be about members of the same family, for example, or about three friends. They might be about different people at the same location, or three people taking part in the same sport. There are many possibilities, of course. Use your imagination.

Answer key
Clapping for the clerihew

Answers will vary. Here is an example:

Cali the Cat is phenomenal.
She thinks that dogs are abominable.
I must confido
She beats any Fido.

Bonus

Answers will vary. Here are three examples on the subject of school sports:

When our team plays basketball, Melanie
sweats so bad it's a felony.
But after she takes a shower,
she smells as good as a gigantic flower.

Our coach, Mrs. Harris,
stands on the sideline looking embarrassed.
With that whistle permanently jammed in her mouth,
she thinks she has a lot of clout.

The cheerleader Betsy Moreno
says she would rather be in a casino
than on this stupid court
wearing a skirt that is way too short.

Lora P.

August

Where is it?

The United States has more national parks than many people imagine. Most people know about the major ones, like Yellowstone and the Grand Canyon. However, there are many, many more parks across the country, as well as national monuments, preserves, historic sites, historic parks, memorials, battlefields, cemeteries, recreation areas, seashores, lakeshores, rivers, parkways, trails and other designations — all within the National Park System. In honor of National Parks Month, match each unit in the National Park System below with the state where it's located. (All but four states are represented.)

1. Carlsbad Caverns National Park _____

2. Edison National Historic Site _____

3. Fire Island National Seashore _____

4. Cape Hatteras National Seashore _____

5. Theodore Roosevelt National Park _____

6. Mound City Group National Monument _____

7. Chickasaw Recreation Area _____

8. Crater Lake National Park _____

9. Valley Forge National Historical Park _____

10. Fort Sumter National Monument _____

11. Badlands National Park _____

12. Great Smoky Mountains National Park _____

13. Arches National Park _____

14. Shenandoah National Park _____

15. Mount Rainier National Park _____

16. Harpers Ferry National Historic Park _____

17. Apostle Islands National Lakeshore _____

18. Effigy Mounds National Monument _____

19. Fort Scott National Historic Site _____

20. Mammoth Cave National Park _____

21. Jean Lafitte National Historical Park and Preserve _____

22. Acadia National Park _____

23. Assateague Island National Seashore _____

24. Cape Cod National Seashore _____

25. Pictured Rocks National Lakeshore _____

26. Voyageurs National Park _____

27. Natchez Trace Parkway _____

28. Harry S. Truman National Historic Site _____

29. Agate Fossil Beds National Monument _____

30. Great Basin National Park _____

31. Saint-Gaudens National Historic Site _____

32. Grand Teton
    National Park _____

33. Grand Canyon
    National Park _____

34. Rocky Mountain
    National Park _____

35. Yosemite National Park _____

36. Big Bend National Park _____

37. Everglades National Park _____

38. Hot Springs National Park _____

39. Glacier National Park _____

40. The White House _____

41. Denali National Park
    and Preserve _____

42. Haleakala National Park _____

43. Craters of the Moon
    National Monument _____

44. Tuskegee Institute National Historic
    Site _____

45. Martin Luther King, Jr., National Historic Site _____

46. Lincoln Home
    National Historic Site _____

47. Indiana Dunes
    National Lakeshore _____

States

Alabama	Indiana	Nebraska	South Carolina
Alaska	Iowa	Nevada	South Dakota
Arizona	Kansas	New Hampshire	Tennessee
Arkansas	Kentucky	New Jersey	Texas
California	Louisiana	New Mexico	Utah
Colorado	Maine	New York	Vermont
Connecticut	Maryland	North Carolina	Virginia
Delaware	Massachusetts	North Dakota	Washington
Florida	Michigan	Ohio	Washington, D.C.
Georgia	Minnesota	Oklahoma	West Virginia
Hawaii	Mississippi	Oregon	Wisconsin
Idaho	Missouri	Pennsylvania	Wyoming
Illinois	Montana	Rhode Island	

Bonus

Do one of the following:

- Make a wildlife or botanical poster for one of the parks above. Include at least 10 animals or 10 plants that live in the park. Use pictures and brief descriptions for each animal or plant.

- Write a letter to the principal persuading him or her that your class should take a field trip to one of the parks. Include specific features about the park that you think might be educational.

Answer key
Where is it?

1. New Mexico
2. New Jersey
3. New York
4. North Carolina
5. North Dakota
6. Ohio
7. Oklahoma
8. Oregon
9. Pennsylvania
10. South Carolina
11. South Dakota
12. Tennessee
13. Utah
14. Virginia
15. Washington
16. West Virginia
17. Wisconsin
18. Iowa
19. Kansas
20. Kentucky
21. Louisiana
22. Maine
23. Maryland
24. Massachusetts
25. Michigan
26. Minnesota
27. Mississippi
28. Missouri
29. Nebraska
30. Nevada
31. New Hampshire
32. Wyoming
33. Arizona
34. Colorado
35. California
36. Texas
37. Florida
38. Arkansas
39. Montana
40. Washington, D.C.
41. Alaska
42. Hawaii
43. Idaho
44. Alabama
45. Georgia
46. Illinois
47. Indiana

Bonus

Answers will vary. Here is one example:

Dear Ms. McGraw:

Our class would like to go on a field trip to Grand Teton National Park because we are all living in Brooklyn and never get to see wild moose and elk. I read about this park and found out there are lots of wild animals and lakes and mountains. Our class has been studying the West, and there is a lot of history about the West in Jackson, Wyoming, which is right by Grand Teton National Park. We could stay in tents and camp in the park and learn to make camp fires. We would also be saving money by not staying in hotels.

If you let us go, we promise to do a report with pictures and stories of our trip to share with the rest of the school.

Sincerely,

Jeff B.
Mrs. Ward's 8th grade social studies class

Showing some teeth

In honor of National Smile Week (the first Monday through Sunday of August), think about what makes *you* smile. Take some time, and see if you can come up with 30 things.

Remember, your list will be unique to you. What makes you smile might not make someone else smile. That's okay.

Examples

Little kittens playing
Toddlers running away from their parents at the mall
Mocha fudge ice cream

What makes me smile:

1. _____
2. _____
3. _____
4. _____
5. _____
6. _____
7. _____
8. _____
9. _____
10. _____
11. _____
12. _____
13. _____
14. _____
15. _____
16. _____
17. _____
18. _____
19. _____
20. _____
21. _____
22. _____
23. _____
24. _____
25. _____
26. _____
27. _____
28. _____
29. _____
30. _____

Post your list in a place where you will see it frequently. If you feel down in the dumps, look at your list. Sometimes just *thinking* about the items on the list will make you smile.

Also, try to arrange your life so that you will encounter what makes you smile. If it's kittens playing, and you haven't seen any in a while, maybe it's time for a trip to a pet store. People who do and see what makes them happy find themselves feeling happy.

Answer key
Showing some teeth

Answers will vary. Here are some possibilities:

1. babies grabbing my finger
2. the old "Dick Van Dyke Show"
3. the little kids on "Rug Rats"
4. an old man with his arm around his wife
5. kids playing in those bins of plastic balls at McDonald's
6. great clothes on sale
7. a check in the mail
8. the "One Big Happy" cartoon strip
9. penguins
10. rose gardens in bloom
11. taking off in an airplane
12. when someone else does the dishes
13. getting phone calls
14. listening to a new CD
15. eating a popsicle when it's hot outside
16. swimming at night
17. watching the Olympics
18. being barefoot
19. the word "reckon"
20. the smell of suntan lotion
21. denim overalls
22. kittens
23. pizza with sausage and mushrooms
24. ice cream cones
25. leafy trees hanging over the road
26. camping
27. my baby brother with pudding all over his face
28. my grandma's potato pancakes
29. fireworks
30. the Pacific Ocean

What's your sign?

August 1, 1981, marked the debut of MTV. If you have ever watched MTV for any length of time, you have probably noticed the MTV logo. The logo design appears in every form imaginable, from gross to funny. One day the letters in the design might appear to be made from a bologna sandwich on white bread. The next day the logo might look as though it is made from a tooth recently removed by a dentist.

Using your own initials, make an MTV-style logo for yourself. Then take your logo and have some fun with it, just as MTV does with its logo. You might draw on it, paste things on it or mold it out of something from home, for example.

There are only two requirements for your design:

- Make it fit your personality or represent *you* in some way.
- The more unusual it is, the better. (For example, one student, a bicycle fanatic, made a logo out of different colored tire marks from his bicycle.)

When you finish your design, write a brief paragraph that explains why you did what you did.

Answer key
What's your sign?

Answers will vary. Here is one possibility:

I did this drawing of a football player because I play football, and I love it. My name is Zachary Allan Howard, so my initials are Z.A.H. The padded shoulders of my logo help form the "Z".

Trapped!

Have you ever noticed how television shows are always trapping characters together on elevators? In fact, when you see people getting onto an elevator on a television show, you can be pretty sure that the elevator is going to stop between floors, especially if the people are fighting or don't like each other. It's a very common story device — probably because the results can be very interesting.

In honor of the invention of the elevator, on August 2, 1743, and in honor of all that **tr**apping, look at the trapped elevator below. See if you can find at least 36 items that begin with the letters "tr."

Answer key
Trapped!

1. tricycle
2. troll
3. triangle
4. trigonometry book
5. triceratops
6. trapeze artist
7. trophy
8. tree
9. trunk
10. traveler
11. traveler's checks
12. trial jury
13. Trojan horse
14. triplets
15. troubadours
16. trumpet
17. track shoes
18. treble clef
19. truffle
20. treat
21. trombone
22. trousers
23. traffic light
24. trout
25. tropical fish
26. tribe
27. treaty
28. tripod
29. treasure
30. tracks
31. train
32. trampoline
33. Trivial Pursuit game
34. truck
35. trash bags
36. tractor trailer

If I only had a brain

In the classic movie, *The Wizard of Oz*, the scarecrow wants a brain, and the tin man wants a heart. If you were going to request an additional body part from the Wizard of Oz, what part would it be? (Make it a public body part, please!) Would another arm be helpful? Another thumb? A mouth lock that automatically snaps into place whenever you are about to say something stupid?

Write your request to the wizard, and persuade him to grant your request.

_____
_____
_____
_____
_____
_____
_____
_____
_____
_____
_____
_____
_____
_____
_____
_____
_____
_____
_____
_____
_____
_____
_____
_____

Answer key
If I only had a brain

Answers will vary. Here is one example:

Dear Mr. Wizard:

I am so happy you decided to get a mailing address. The yellow brick road is full of pot holes and needs to be repaved.

The reason I'm writing is to request another right hand. Now that I'm in seventh grade, my teachers give me so much homework that my hand starts aching before I'm even halfway finished with my work. If I had another right hand, I could keep up with all my homework and get the straight *A*'s I deserve. There's something else, too. Could you make it detachable? That way, I can remove it when I'm ready to do something else, like play soccer or go swimming.

Thank you, sir, for your kind attention. I'll send my measurements and specifications as soon as I hear from you.

Sincerely,

Ethan R.

Roller coaster ride

Where do we find roller coasters? In an amusement park, of course. And what else do we find in an amusement park? Zillions of things, like cotton candy, popcorn, children, oil and grease for the rides, tennis shoes, bumper cars, french fries and hamburgers.

Make a list of everything you can think of that might be found in an amusement park. When you have a long list, fit the words into the roller coaster puzzle below. The last letter of the first word should be the *first* letter of the next word. The last letter of that word should be the first letter of the next word, and so forth.

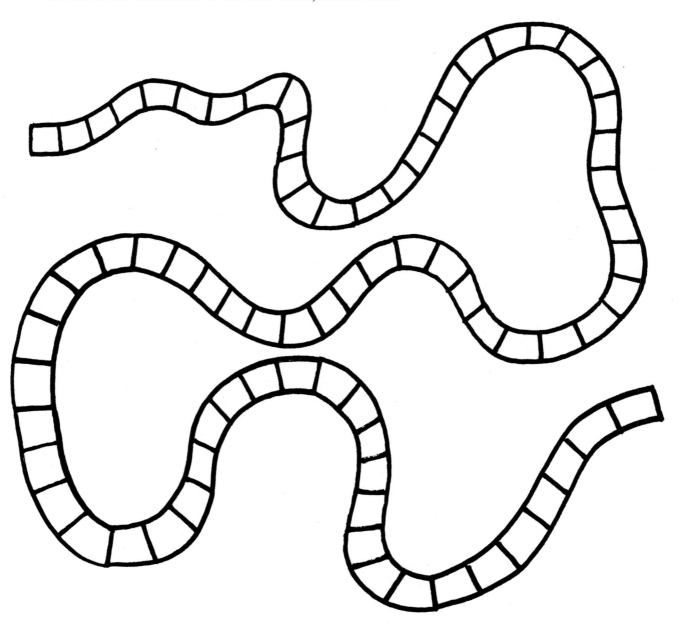

Answer key
Roller coaster ride

Answers will vary. Here is one solution:

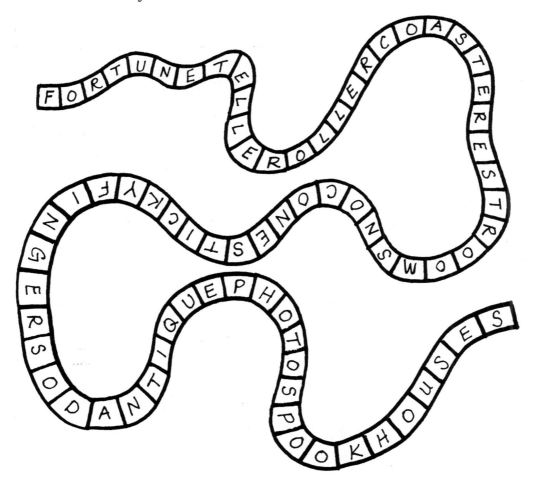

Create a holiday

Perhaps no one you know celebrates Sauerkraut Salad and Sandwich Season. (Actually, some people believe *no one* in his right mind celebrates Sauerkraut Salad and Sandwich Season!) However, the National Kraut Packers Association has decided that America should launch the outdoor eating season with sauerkraut sandwiches and salads.

If the National Kraut Packers Association can come up with a special season, so can you. Just for fun, come up with ten ideas for holidays that probably *won't* sweep America but that *you* think should be celebrated.

For example, one person might want October to be National Borrow Whatever Clothes You Want From Your Sister Month. Someone whose favorite food is mashed potatoes might decide that her birthday, March 11, should be National Mashed Potato Day.

List your potential holidays below.

1. _____
2. _____
3. _____
4. _____
5. _____
6. _____
7. _____
8. _____
9. _____
10. _____

Bonus

Now pick one holiday and describe how it should be celebrated. Perhaps you will want to choose a figure to represent your holiday, as cupid sometimes represents Valentine's Day or a leprechaun sometimes represents Saint Patrick's Day.

Answer key
Create a holiday

Answers will vary. Here are some possibilities:

January — Dream of Sunny Summer Days Month
February 20 — National Cats Are People Too Day
April — No Math Homework Month
June 20 — National Take Your Dog to the Park and Throw a Frisbee Day
August 10-14 — Learn the Dangers of Brussels Sprouts Week
October 19 — International Eat Banana Popsicles Day
December — All Brothers Must Do What Their Sisters Tell Them Month

Bonus

Answers will vary. Here is one example:

For Learn the Dangers of Brussels
Sprouts Week (August 10-14),
I would use the symbol on the
right:

I'd celebrate the holiday like this:

August 10 — Show pictures of people injured by brussels sprouts
August 11 — Broadcast the dangers of brussels sprouts (They can explode, for example, causing injuries.)
August 12 — Have a community picnic. Serve no brussels sprouts.
August 13 — Prepare recipes using no brussels sprouts.
August 14 — Give medals to people who have avoided all brussels sprouts for an entire year.

Artie A.

September

Coat it with honey

When parents want their children to take terrible-tasting medicine, they sometimes mix it with a thick tablespoon of honey. The honey makes the bitter medicine go down easier.

Sometimes words can be coated with honey, too — in other words, sometimes we can say something more "sweetly" in order to take the unpleasantness out of the meaning.

For example, a mother might say, "Take out the trash. NOW!" If she wanted to coat the words with honey, she might say, "Sweetheart, it's time for you to snuggle up to that bag of garbage. I'm sure you will do it right away, since you know I need this kitchen cleared out."

If a father is letting his daughter borrow the car, he might say, "Bring it back FULL of gas." If he wanted to make his words honey-coated, he could say something like this: "I'm just as happy as can be to let you borrow my car, especially because I know what a considerate person you are. I know you wouldn't THINK of bringing that car back without having the tank full."

You get the idea. In honor of National Honey Month, try your hand at coating the following statements with honey. Really lay it on. Be sweet!

1. I wouldn't go out with you if you were the last person on earth. _____
_____
_____

2. No, I don't want any spinach. Spinach makes me throw up. _____
_____
_____

3. Please don't make me take algebra. I HATE math. _____
_____
_____

4. Get over here and help me clean up these dishes. _____
_____
_____

5. Of course you can't borrow my shirt. Absolutely NOT! _____
_____
_____

6. You're fired! _____
_____
_____

7. No, you can't have a pony! Are you crazy? _____
_____
_____

8. That dress makes you look fat. _____
_____

Answer key
Coat it with honey

Answers will vary. Here is one possibility:

1. You and I are just so different from each other. I think we each need someone who would be in a better position to appreciate all we have to offer.
2. Because I know how much you love spinach, I'll let you have my portion.
3. Out of the kindness of my heart, I would gladly help keep class size down by not enrolling in algebra.
4. There is no one else on earth who can clean a dish with the special flair that you have. Therefore, I have selected you to be my special dish assistant, an honor bestowed on only the best and brightest people.
5. It would be horrible of me to let you walk out of here wearing my shirt, which takes your great-looking face and makes it appear totally ordinary.
6. Because of your special talents and abilities, we have decided it's time for you to move on to a company that will be able to take advantage of all you have to offer.
7. I wouldn't want you to have something that would require as much work and attention as a pony, especially with all the important things you have to do. Here's a goldfish.
8. Nothing in the world could make someone with your body look heavy, but that dress certainly doesn't show off your fine figure.

How funky is your chicken?

September is National Chicken Month. If your favorite food is fried chicken, you may have positive thoughts about chickens. However, chickens, in general, have a pretty bad reputation. Think about it:

- People use the term "chicken" for someone they think is a coward.
- Some people refuse to wear shorts because they swear they have "chicken" legs.
- Those who are always nagging and fussing are sometimes called mother "hens."
- And finally what is one of the worst jokes ever — Why did the chicken cross the road?

Clearly, the poor chicken can use an image boost. Imagine that the chickens of the world have hired you as their personal image consultant to help them get rid of their negative image. The chickens have told you that they want to be "cool, funky and hip." They want a radical new look, a new name and a catchy slogan.

Bonus

Write a theme song for the chickens. Use the tune of an existing song and write new lyrics. Or, if you happen to be musical, write your own lyrics *and* melody.

Answer key
How funky is your chicken?

Answers will vary. Here is an example one student came up with:

- New name: "Chic-en," pronounced with a heavy French accent and a stress on the second syllable.

- New motto: The only road *this* chicken crosses is the Champs-Elysées, a street in Paris.

- New look:

- New theme song (sung to the tune of "Frère Jacques"):

Monsieur Chicken, Monsieur Chicken
You're so cool. You're so cool.
The way you cluck all morning,
Your crazy pecking order,
And your beak, and your beak.

Elizabeth D.

Not for a million dollars

Labor Day is a holiday set aside to honor working people and labor unions. It also marks the unofficial end of summer.

In honor of Labor Day, think about your future. Adults are always asking young people, "What do you want to be when you grow up?" They never ask, "What is it that you DON'T want to be?"

Most young people have a very good idea of what they would be absolutely miserable doing. For example, Max hates sitting down and being inside all day. He would never ever want to have an office job. Alicia hates the sight of blood and knows she would never ever want to be a doctor or a nurse.

What do you know that you would never ever — not for all the money in the world — choose as a job or career? Write about what you would never do. How do you think such work would make you feel? Why would you never want to do it?

_____

_____

_____

_____

_____

_____

_____

_____

_____

_____

_____

_____

_____

_____

_____

_____

_____

_____

_____

_____

_____

Answer key
Not for a million dollars

Answers will vary. Here is one example:

I would really hate to be a truck driver. I get sick in cars, so driving across country doesn't appeal to me. I really wouldn't want to drive down the road staring at pavement for miles and miles. Also, I really hate traffic. If the traffic is bad in the cities, a truck driver has to sit in a big hot truck listening to cars blaring in his ear while he inches forward for an hour, just to get about half a mile. Finally, for all the trouble they go through to get the supplies to their destination, truck drivers don't get all that much money — only about $25,000 a year, according to a show I saw on TV. That's just not enough if you have a family.

Zachary H.

Teams in disguise

Below are the disguised names of 30 professional football teams. In honor of the anniversary of the first professional football game, see if you can match the disguised names with the actual team names.

Disguised team names

_____1) Fast flyers
_____2) Swashbucklers
_____3) Mane men of the jungle
_____4) Heifer lads
_____5) Suitcase fillers
_____6) Rent, cable, electric and heat invoices
_____7) Beanstalk dwellers
_____8) High flying hunters
_____9) Credit card users
_____10) Dark and vivid reds
_____11) Intentional colliders
_____12) Scandanavian explorers
_____13) Sea villains
_____14) Bald birds
_____15) Flipper's relatives
_____16) Black birds associated with Edgar Allan Poe
_____17) Expensive, fast cars
_____18) Thieves
_____19) Tin man fixers
_____20) Young horses
_____21) Sleek black jungle cats
_____22) Ocean birds
_____23) Holy people
_____24) Wild or semi-wild horses
_____25) Defenders of their country
_____26) Pillagers
_____27) Cousins of Frosted Flakes spokesman
_____28) hibernating huckleberry eaters

Real team names

A. Packers
B. Cowboys
C. Chargers
D. Giants
E. Rams
F. Steelers
G. Pirates
H. Eagles
I. Ravens
J. Dolphins
K. Jets
L. Raiders
M. Cardinals
N. Lions
O. Broncos
P. Bills
Q. Seahawks
R. Panthers
S. Jaguars
T. Vikings
U. Oilers
V. Bengals
W. Patriots
X. Falcons
Y. Colts
Z. Bears
AA. Saints
BB. Buccaneers

Answer key
Teams in disguise

1. K
2. BB
3. N
4. B
5. A
6. P
7. D
8. X
9. C
10. M
11. E
12. T
13. G
14. H
15. J
16. I
17. S
18. F
19. U
20. Y
21. R
22. Q
23. AA
24. O
25. W
26. L
27. V
28. Z

There ought to be a law!

On September 4, 1961, the hijacking of airplanes was outlawed. You may wonder why it took so long to outlaw such a dangerous activity. Sometimes lawmakers have their hands full and just can't get around to making all the laws we may need.

Write out ten new laws that *you* think should be on the books. Be as silly or as serious as you wish, but be prepared to defend your idea for new legislation.

Examples

No telephone solicitation
No mowing your lawn before noon on weekends
Movie theaters cannot charge more than two dollars for a soft drink.

After you have your laws written, decide upon a proper and fitting penalty for the violation of each law. (Keep in mind the Eighth Amendment, which prohibits cruel and unusual punishment!) Try to make your punishment fit the crime. If a theater owner violates a law against charging more than two dollars for a soft drink at a movie theater, for example, the penalty might be for the person to drink a gallon of the soft drink, after it has been sitting outside for three days and gone flat.

1. _____
   _____
2. _____
   _____
3. _____
   _____
4. _____
   _____
5. _____
   _____
6. _____
   _____
7. _____
   _____
8. _____
   _____
9. _____
   _____
10. _____
   _____

Answer key
There ought to be a law!

Answers will vary. Here are some possibilities:

1. Mothers cannot make their children eat liver. If they do, they have to dab liver juice behind their ears like perfume and wear it for a week.

2. Fathers cannot make their kids wash their cars. If they do, they have to wash their kids' bikes every day for one month.

3. Parents can't yell at their kids for eating at the computer. If they do, they have to eat their dinner in the car that night.

4. Principals have to let kids wear shorts to school. If they don't, they have to wear cut-offs and flip flops with a shirt and tie every day for a month. Also, they can't have an air conditioner in their office.

5. Principals cannot speak over the intercom for more than three minutes a day. If they do, they have to listen to Megadeth through a Walkman all day long.

6. Teachers can't intercept students' notes in class. If they do, then they have to read two pages from their own diary to the whole class.

7. People have to recycle everything that is recyclable. If they don't, they have to bury all their trash in their own front yard for one month.

8. Parents can't automatically make their daughters (and not their sons) do the dishes. If they do, they have to triple their daughters' allowances.

9. Libraries cannot charge you for something that's only a couple days overdue. If they do, the librarian has to count and roll all the pennies you have been saving since the second grade.

10. People can't keep their dogs tied up all day. If they do, they have to clean all the cages at the dog pound for ten years. Then they have to spend a month living in a cage at the dog pound.

All in a name

On September 9, 1776, the founders of our country gave it the name United States of America. Most of us rarely call our country by its full name. Sometimes we say *America* and sometimes we say *United States*.

We also seldom stop to consider that there is some controversy about using the term "*American*" to mean only residents of the United States. In fact, people in *all* the countries of North and South America can call themselves Americans.

We could always call ourselves U.S. citizens, but that term often seems cumbersome. We could invent a word like *United Statesian*, but that seems awkward, too.

Suppose that the founders of the United States had the chance to name our country all over again, this time choosing a different name. What name would you suggest? Why? While you are at it, try thinking of new names for *all* of the places below. Be sure to explain the reason for each new name.

1. United States of America _____

   _____

   _____

   _____

2. Your state _____

   _____

   _____

3. Your city/town _____

   _____

   _____

4. The street you live on _____

   _____

   _____

5. The earth _____

   _____

   _____

6. The sun _____

   _____

   _____

Answer key
All in a name

Answers will vary. Here are a few possibilities:

1. United States of America — I would rename it Diversia. I would call it this because we have such a diverse population with so many kinds of people.

2. Your state — I would rename Colorado "Prism" because it is so colorful with its evergreens, big blue skies and gold-filled mountains.

3. Your city/town — I would call my town "Middle Track" because a train track goes right through the middle of town.

4. The street you live on — I would name my street Lilac Lane because there are so many lilacs and lilac-colored flowers that border the street.

5. The earth — I'd call the earth "Gaea." All the other planets are named after something in mythology. Gaea was mother of the earth, and so I thought she would be a good choice.

6. The sun — I would call it Marigold because it looks like a big golden marigold in full bloom.

Double overtime

The third Saturday in September is the first day of National Sports Junkie Week. To celebrate, try the challenge below, using only words from the field of sports. You may include names of teams, last names of famous individuals from various sports, and sports terms.

Example

List three 3-letter words:
out, hit, net

1. List four 4-letter words. _____
_____
_____

2. List five 5-letter words. _____
_____
_____

3. List six 6-letter words. _____
_____
_____

4. List seven 7-letter words. _____
_____
_____

5. List eight 8-letter words. _____
_____
_____

6. List nine 9-letter words. _____
_____
_____

7. List ten 10-letter words. _____
_____
_____

Answer key
Double overtime

Answers will vary. Here are some possibilities:

1. goal, ball, Cubs, swim
2. Lions, skate, spare, serve, slope
3. Jordan, strike, tennis, racket, inning, hockey
4. Packers, Yankees, Gretzky, javelin, Stanley, bowling, stadium
5. marathon, swimming, baseball, knockout, Olympics, Mariners, Andretti, Louganis
6. backboard, Yamaguchi, Avalanche, Cardinals, Wimbledon, wrestling, announcer, badminton, athletics
7. volleyball, basketball, heptathlon, gymnastics, scoreboard, Buccaneers, trampoline, equestrian, pentathlon, backstroke

October

Tick tock

In honor of National Clock Month, complete the puzzle below. For each item, find a word that fits the definition and contains "tic" or "toc."

Example
We used a _____stick_____ for roasting marshmallows.

1. Sometimes a pond is _____ with fish.

2. Adults often make babies laugh by _____ them.

3. Most states require an automobile safety _____on the windshield.

4. Caramel apples are very _____ .

5. With high heels, most women wear nylon _____ .

6. Concert _____ for big stars are very expensive and hard to get.

7. Walk softly, but carry a big _____ .

8. At my house, we store all the Christmas stuff in the _____ .

9. If you damage your _____ nerve, you may not be able to see.

10. Another word for *artificial* is _____ .

11. When he sent me flowers after I broke my leg, I could tell he was very _____ .

12. He worked on an exercise machine every day to trim his _____ .

Bonus

See if you can add three items of your own to the puzzle above. Be sure to include an answer key.

1. _____

2. _____

3. _____

Answer key
Tick tock

1. stocked
2. tickling
3. sticker
4. sticky
5. stockings
6. tickets
7. stick
8. attic
9. optic
10. synthetic
11. sympathetic
12. buttocks

Bonus

1. If you want to learn a trade, you should become an (apprentice).
2. It's hard to understand the disc jockey since this radio has so much (static).
3. Anyone who has taken care of a three-year-old knows that they are very (energetic).

Peter Piper picked a peck

Nearly everyone has heard the old tongue twister that begins, "Peter Piper picked a peck of pickled peppers . . . " What makes the tongue twister difficult to say is all the *alliteration*. Alliteration is the repetition of the same consonant sound, in this case, "p."

In honor of National Pickled Pepper Week (the week of the first two weekends of October, from Friday through Monday), try some alliteration of your own. Write 20 *alliterative* sentences, all involving food.

Examples

Dress up dessert with delicious dates.
Ruth is ready to read a remarkable raisin recipe.

1. _____
2. _____
3. _____
4. _____
5. _____
6. _____
7. _____
8. _____
9. _____
10. _____
11. _____
12. _____
13. _____
14. _____
15. _____
16. _____
17. _____
18. _____
19. _____
20. _____

Answer key
Peter Piper picked a peck

Answers will vary. Here are some possibilities:

1. Zachary was zooming around a zany zucchini patch.
2. Garth was gorging on groovy grapes.
3. Clara was counting out cups of colossal corn.
4. Yolanda was yearning for yummy yams.
5. The Matthews munched on mysterious meatloaf every Monday..
6. Tom took the tops off tons of tantalizing tomatoes.
7. Carrie cut up crates of cool cantaloupes.
8. Waldo wanted to win a whopping watermelon.
9. Al Amundson appreciates appetizing apples.
10. Melissa was marinating mountains of marvelous mutton.
11. Helping happy folks eat hearty, huge hamburgers was Henry's hobby.
12. Casey cooked a kettle of crunchy carrots.
13. Selling salty taffy at the seashore sweetened Sally's summer.
14. David dribbled dollops of dressing at dinner.
15. Eartha, at eighteen, eats eggplant every evening.
16. Penelope pondered politics as she picked at her plate of pasta primavera.
17. Chris crept across the carpet, crunching crispy cookies.
18. Daniel dipped his dentures in his Diet Dr Pepper at dinner.
19. Thomas tripped while taking the tantalizing tamales to the Thompsons' table.
20. Samantha spit her squishy sushi at her sister Sara.

Words in common

People everywhere take words for granted. We use them without even thinking about them. We take advantage of them. We don't stop and think about how useful they are in our everyday life.

Newspapers are, of course, full of words. That's why it is appropriate to celebrate *words* during National Newspaper Week. One way to celebrate words is to honor the words we use the most. Can you guess what they might be?

The most common words used by the average English speaker are these:

the	to	that	it
of	a	is	for
and	in	I	as

Obviously, these aren't the most exciting words in the world (although we all have a fondness for "I"). They are, however, awfully important. To gain an appreciation of these words, try writing a sentence on each of the subjects below *without* using any of the above words.

Example

Subject: television
*My favorite television show, **NYPD Blue**, comes on at 9:00.*

1. Subject: sports _____
   _____

2. Subject: pets _____
   _____

3. Subject: spiders _____
   _____

4. Subject: cars _____
   _____

5. Subject: school _____
   _____

6. Subject: shopping _____
   _____

7. Subject: fast food _____
   _____

8. Subject: pet peeve _____
   _____

Answer key
Words in common

Answers will vary. Here are some possibilities:

1. Bowling alley sounds drive me crazy.
2. Our two dogs cannot stop chasing squirrels, no matter what we do.
3. Whenever Bonnie sees spiders, she screams with fright.
4. Mario's old yellow Volkswagen just keeps on running.
5. Biology lab produces weird odors on Thursday afternoons.
6. Grocery stores need wider aisles on Saturday afternoons.
7. Unfortunately, those burgers John eats each night look greasy.
8. She hates how my sister snaps her gum so loudly.

Triple word challenge

In honor of Dictionary Day, complete the triple word challenge below. For each item, write one sentence that makes sense and includes all three words listed. Unless you have an unusually large vocabulary, a dictionary will be helpful.

One more note: The sentences must show the meaning of the words. It is NOT okay to write a sentence like this one: *Chary, chassé and chase are three words I don't know.*

Example

Chary, Chassé, Chase:
*The dancer was **chary** of performing her **chassé** after hurting her ankle in the **chase** to catch the bank robber.*

1. gaunt, gauze, garret _____

   _____

2. halitosis, hallucinate, haggard _____

   _____

3. maunder, mazer, mazurka _____

   _____

4. palaver, pannier, pantry _____

   _____

5. saltation, sanatorium, sapid _____

   _____

6. streusel, succor, sundries _____

   _____

7. tacit, tact, taffeta _____

   _____

8. virago, virus, visage _____

   _____

Bonus

Add at least one item to the puzzle above. Be sure to include an answer key.

Answer key
Triple word challenge

Answers will vary. Here are some possibilities:

1. The artist appeared **gaunt** after he emerged from the **garret**, wearing a **gauze** pad over the cut on his forehead.
2. The dentist recommended mints for Fred's **halitosis**, but the **hallucinations** they gave him left him looking **haggard**.
3. In the early morning, Barb would often **maunder** as she poured her coffee in the **mazer** while a **mazurka** played loudly in the background.
4. The women engaged in **palaver** as Meredith retrieved her **pannier** from the **pantry**.
5. Upon his release from the **sanatorium**, Jonathon engaged in **saltation** as he tasted the **sapid** berries.
6. The **streusel** provided **succor** when the shop owner found the **sundries** stolen from the shelves.
7. Bob and Brian made a **tacit** agreement to use **tact** in describing Andrea's **taffeta** gown.
8. The **visage** on the **virago** spoke volumes about the pain caused by her **virus**.

Bonus

Answers will vary. One possibility:

yammer, yak, yacht
James **yammered** at the **yak** as he tried to yank it onto the **yacht**.

Riding in luxury

On October 17, 1902, the first Cadillac car was completed in Detroit, Michigan. The Cadillac eventually became a symbol of luxury for many Americans. People who had "made it" had a Cadillac.

Of course, tastes differ. Perhaps your idea of a luxury car is something else entirely. Suppose that people were able to hire car designers to design their dream cars, just as they sometimes hire architects to design their dream homes. What would your dream car be like? Describe it in detail.

Bonus

Draw a picture of your dream car.

Answer key
Riding in luxury

My dream car can go 150 miles per hour. It is a convertible sports car/limousine with an enormous easy chair in the back. It also has a really great, loud stereo system and a big trunk that can hold lots of camping gear. I can put my car into four-wheel drive to go through snow and mud and over huge boulders. A chauffeur can drive my car if I want to lounge in the easy chair. Or, if I want to drive, the easy chair scoots forward and shrinks into a normal driver's seat.

Dave M.

Bonus

Holy hippo

In 1938, Chester Carlson, inventor of xerography, made the first photocopy at his lab in Astoria, New York. In honor of Carlson, the Xerox Corporation has designated October 22 as Copycat Day.

"Copycat" is a common term in our language, but where did the term originate? Cats don't really copy each other, any more than any other animal. Even when it is not easy to see the connection, people often use animals to describe the peculiarities of people. Some of the phrases become adopted into our language, and people use them without even thinking about them.

The letter that follows is written by LuAnn, one of those people who is always getting her phrases mixed up, using the wrong animals. Decipher the story by circling all the animal phrases used incorrectly. Write in the correct animal above each phrase.

Dear Katy:

You asked me to tell you how your Grandpa Bob and Grandma Eudora finally got married. Your Grandpa Bob was as sly as a **sheep**. Holy **hippo**! Let me tell you the story.

You see, Eudora's father, Zebediah, did not like your Grandpa Bob one bit. Zebediah worked at the saw mill and was strong as a **tick**. Bob, on the other hand, was a skinny, little book**walrus** who was as quiet as a **loon**. In the mill town where they lived, Bob was kind of a **chimpanzee** out of water. Zebediah thought Eudora should be with someone strong like him. Despite her pleas, he was as stubborn as a **flamingo** on the subject. He told her it was just **porpoise** love and that when she grew up she would realize she was making a grave mistake.

For a while the two tried to date each other on the sly, but old Zebediah had eyes like a **rhinoceros** and saw everything that went on. Bob loved Eudora so much that he knew they had to devise a plan to run off to the next town and be married. However, they knew that the second Zebediah found out, he would run after them quick as a **platypus**. So, they decided to send him on a wild **moose** chase.

Eudora left a note for her father, Zebediah, telling him that she was hiding because Bob had broken her heart and left her for another girl in town. She told Zebediah not to come after her because she was too ashamed to see anyone. After reading that note, Zebediah was as grumpy as a **tadpole**. He was so mad his face turned red as an **ostrich**. He thought to himself, "That jerk Bob is like a **boar** leaving a sinking ship." Zebediah ran around town looking for Bob. He wanted to clobber him for breaking his daughter's heart. He looked and looked everywhere for the boy, until he was **antelope** tired and just couldn't go on.

When he came home, Zebediah saw both Eudora and Bob sitting on the porch holding hands and looking about as happy as a **hammerhead shark**. Eudora ran up to him and explained, "Dad we didn't mean to trick you, and please don't have an **orangutan**, but Bob and I ran off and got married. I hope you'll understand someday."

At first Zebediah was really angry, but as the evening went on, he realized he had been wrong. He told them, "Now you know I can be proud as a **zebra** sometimes, so this is hard for me to say. I must have been as blind as a **giraffe** not to see how happy you two little love **pandas** are. You two have my blessing."

And they all three lived happily ever after.

Love,

Aunt LuAnn

Bonus

Now write another Aunt LuAnn letter with mixed up animal phrases and sentences. See if you can use at least 10 well-known animal phrases in your story. (Be sure to include an answer key.) Here are a few ideas:

Birds of a feather flock together.
You can lead a horse to water but you can't make him drink.
a wolf in sheep's clothing
playing possum
Don't put the cart before the horse.
Don't count your chickens before they hatch.
proud as a peacock
eats like a horse
Curiosity killed the cat.

Answer key
Holy hippo

Dear Katy,

You asked me to tell you how your Grandpa Bob and Grandma Eudora finally got married. Your Grandpa Bob was as sly as a **fox**. Holy **cow**! Let me tell you the story.

You see, Eudora's father, Zebediah, did not like your Grandpa Bob one bit. Zebediah worked at the saw mill and was strong as an **ox**. Bob, on the other hand, was a skinny, little book**worm** who was as quiet as a **mouse**. In the mill town where they lived, Bob was kind of a **fish** out of water. Zebediah thought Eudora should be with someone strong like him. Despite her pleas, he was as stubborn as a **mule** on the subject. He told her it was just **puppy** love and that when she grew up she would realize she had made a grave mistake.

For a while the two tried to date each other on the sly, but old Zebediah had eyes like a **hawk** and saw everything that went on. Bob loved Eudora so much that he knew they had to devise a plan to run off to the next town and be married. However, they knew that the second Zebediah found out, he would run after them quick as a **rabbit**. So, they decided to send him on a wild **goose** chase.

Eudora left a note for her father, Zebediah, telling him that she was hiding because Bob had broken her heart and left her for another girl in town. She told Zebediah not to come after her because she was too ashamed to see anyone. After reading that note, Zebediah was as grumpy as a **bear**. He was so mad his face turned red as a **lobster**. He thought to himself, "That jerk Bob is like a **rat** leaving a sinking ship." Zebediah ran around town looking for Bob. He wanted to clobber him for breaking his daughter's heart. He looked and looked everywhere for the boy, until he was **dog** tired and just couldn't go on.

When he came home, Zebediah saw both Eudora and Bob sitting on the porch holding hands and looking about as happy as a **lark**. Eudora ran up to him and explained, "Dad we didn't mean to trick you, and please don't have a **cow**, but Bob and I ran off and got married. I hope you'll understand someday."

At first Zebediah was really angry, but as the evening went on, he realized he had been wrong. He told them, "Now you know I can be proud as a **peacock** sometimes, so this is hard for me to say. I must have been blind as a **bat** not to see how happy you two little love**birds** are. You two have my blessing."

And they all three lived happily ever after.

Love,
Aunt LuAnn

Bonus

Dear Gus,

Your Aunt Judy was telling me about her stepdaughter Trisha's boyfriend. Alan is over for dinner almost every night and eats like a **whale**. She can hardly keep food in the house. Alan is very different from Trisha's previous boyfriend, who ate like a **kangaroo**. There were always snacks left when he went home.

Trisha and Alan went on a wild **elephant** chase last night. They were looking for just the right wacky birthday gift for a friend. (You know how **gophers** of a feather flock together.) They came home just **zebra** tired with nothing to show for it.

I don't want to let the **puppy** out of the bag, but Aunt Judy thinks Alan is very nice. He is also clever as an **alligator**. Trisha seems as happy as a **horse**. Aunt Judy doesn't want to count her **penguins** before they hatch. She hopes he is not a **lion** in sheep's clothing.

We'll see you next week on our visit.

Love,
Aunt LuAnn

List mania

See if you can complete the following Halloween lists. Title each list, and number the items you include, using your own paper.

1. List 13 well-known monsters.

2. List 13 brand names of candy someone might receive in a trick-or-treat bag.

3. List 13 things that *you* find scary.

4. List 13 nouns that begin with "H" and are at least five letters long.

5. List 13 costumes you are bound to see every Halloween.

6. List 13 adjectives that could sensibly be used instead of the word "scary."

7. List 13 superstitions involving bad luck. (These can be common superstitions, or your own.)

8. List 13 scary movies.

9. List 13 eerie sounds you might hear on Halloween night.

10. List 13 words with a double "e" in them, like "Hallow**ee**n."

11. List 13 words with a double "o" in them, like "Boo!"

12. List 13 things a person might do with a pumpkin.

13. List 13 things that are commonly orange.

Answer key
List mania

Answers will vary. Here are some possibilities:

Monsters
1. Frankenstein
2. Godzilla
3. King Kong
4. Killer Tomatoes
5. Cookie Monster
6. abominable snowman
7. Loch Ness monster
8. Cyclops
9. Dracula
10. Audrey II
11. Cerberus
12. Medusa
13. Minotaur

Candy
1. Hershey Bar
2. Snickers
3. Butterfinger
4. Reese's Pieces
5. Bit O' Honey
6. Nerds
7. Life Savers
8. M & M's
9. Tootsie Roll
10. SweeTarts
11. Skittles
12. Dum-Dums
13. Baby Ruth

Scary things
1. bad drivers
2. plane crashes
3. The Exorcist
4. cancer
5. AIDS
6. serial killers
7. war
8. drowning
9. guns
10. tornadoes
11. vampires
12. spiders
13. rattlesnakes

"H" nouns
1. house
2. horse
3. hyena
4. hangar
5. hippopotamus
6. happiness
7. hockey
8. hierarchy
9. hydrangeas
10. hibiscus
11. hydrogen
12. hamburger
13. hypocrite

Costumes
1. witch
2. ghost
3. pirate
4. devil
5. hobo
6. princess
7. clown
8. ballerina
9. skeleton
10. hippie
11. vampire
12. cheerleader
13. black cat

Adjectives
1. spooky
2. creepy
3. terrifying
4. eerie
5. freaky
6. horrifying
7. ghostly
8. haunted
9. frightening
10. heart-stopping
11. shocking
12. ghastly
13. ghoulish

Superstitions
1. black cat crossing path
2. walking under ladder
3. Friday the 13th
4. breaking mirror
5. spilling salt
6. losing good luck charm
7. too many good things happening
8. someone giving you the evil eye
9. stepping on a crack
10. bringing hail inside brings a hail storm
11. touching a frog causes warts
12. not saying "knock on wood"
13. number 13

Scary movies
1. *Halloween*
2. *Children of the Corn*
3. *Cujo*
4. *Firestarter*
5. *The Exorcist*
6. *Misery*
7. *Pet Sematary*
8. *Friday the 13th*
9. *The Shining*
10. *The Howling*
11. *The Amityville Horror*
12. *Carrie*
13. *Psycho*

Eerie sounds
1. witch cackle
2. black cat meow
3. creaking door
4. clanking chains
5. howling wind
6. thunder
7. ghost moaning
8. bones rattling
9. witches chanting
10. werewolves howling
11. screams
12. organ playing
13. flutter of bat wings

Double "e" words
1. green
2. eerie
3. careen
4. bee
5. spree
6. free
7. Doreen
8. tree
9. flee
10. Beethoven
11. leek
12. week
13. spleen

Double "o" words
1. igloo
2. hullabaloo
3. goo
4. kangaroo
5. moo
6. zoo
7. yoo-hoo
8. stoop
9. too
10. cockatoo
11. achoo
12. shampoo
13. boo hoo

Pumpkin possibilities
1. Make a pumpkin pie.
2. Roast pumpkin seeds.
3. Carve a jack-o-lantern.
4. Use it as part of a Great Pumpkin costume.
5. Use it as a bowling ball.
6. Serve punch in it.
7. Use it as a paper weight.
8. Make an autumn centerpiece with it.
9. Play soccer with it.
10. Use it as a door stop.
11. Get three and use them for juggling.
12. Fill one with Halloween treats.
13. Cook it and eat it like squash.

Orange things
1. pumpkins
2. autumn leaves
3. hats worn for hunting
4. Denver Bronco uniforms
5. detour signs
6. candy corn
7. oranges
8. marigolds
9. one kind of Fruit Loop
10. a car's turn signal
11. clown wig
12. Orange Crush
13. sunsets

November

Wisdom of the ages

A culture's heritage consists of everything it passes down from one generation to the next. This can include traditions, beliefs and even advice. To celebrate Native American Heritage Month, read through the Native American proverbs below. Which ones appeal to you? Which ones puzzle you? Which ones make the most sense to you?

Choose one of the proverbs and write about what it means to you. What advice is it giving? Would you offer the same advice to a friend? Apply the proverb to yourself or to the world around you. Give an example of a situation and tell how the proverb might apply.

- Knowledge that is not used is abused. (Cree)
- Every fire is the same size when it starts. (Seneca)
- Stolen food never satisfies hunger. (Omaha)
- It is easy to be brave from a distance. (Omaha)
- One finger cannot lift a pebble. (Hopi)
- Each bird loves to hear himself sing. (Arapaho)
- We will be known forever by the tracks we leave. (Dakota)
- If you dig a pit for me, you dig one for yourself. (Creole)
- A shady lane breeds mud. (Hopi)
- Always look at your moccasin tracks first before you speak of another's faults. (Sauk)
- The more you ask how far you have to go, the longer your journey seems. (Seneca)
- A spear is a big responsibility. (Navajo)
- The greatest strength is gentleness. (Iroquois)
- Don't let yesterday use up too much of today. (Cherokee)
- The soul would have no rainbow if the eyes had no tears. (Minquass)

Bonus

Select one or more of the proverbs above and make a poster of it, so that others can think about its meaning. Choose a design that fits the message of the proverb.

Answers will vary. Here is one example:

"The soul would have no rainbow if the eyes had no tears." This proverb tells people that crying and feeling sadness are necessary for all human beings. We can't feel great joy and contentment if we can't also feel sorrow. I believe in the idea that we all have a soul that must be cared for. It is our spirit and the essence of our being. The soul can be hidden and damaged when our emotions are not expressed. If we don't let ourselves to cry because of a sad event, our soul will shrivel up because it is not allowed to express itself.

I would give the advice from this proverb to anyone. Sometimes kids try to be tough and pretend they aren't hurt when they really are. For example, my friend acted like it didn't bother her that her parents are getting a divorce. When she stayed overnight with me once, she started talking about it. She cried a lot, and she felt better. I think it's easier to get over things when you can cry about them.

People can get really sick if they never cry when they feel bad. I know that when people get old, they sometimes cry more about things that happened in the past. They have kept their sorrow inside, and no one knew how they felt. My grandfather cries a lot now when he talks about all the friends he saw killed during the Korean War, but my grandmother says he never cried when he first came back from the war. He spent many years feeling bad and never telling anyone about it. It's too bad his soul's rainbow had to wait 50 years to appear.

Sophie K.

"Losers" who weren't

Election Day (the Tuesday after the first Monday in November) always ends with victory celebrations for the winning candidates and the people who supported them. It also ends with sadness and disappointment on the part of the losers and the people who supported them.

What is a "loser" anyway? In popular slang, we talk about "losers" as people who aren't good at anything, who are unpopular, who don't win awards, who don't earn promotions, etc. However, losers in elections are people who have already come a long way being winners. They have won primary elections, a place on the ballot and the confidence of their supporters.

Also, for many losing candidates, being a "loser" is only temporary. Many in history have recovered from devastating election losses, only to be elected President of the United States at a later date. A few examples: Abraham Lincoln, Richard Nixon, Theodore Roosevelt, George Bush, Bill Clinton. Why do some people suffer a loss and then give up? Why do others come back fighting?

Think about *your* definition of a loser. Explain below.

What is a loser?

_____

_____

_____

_____

_____

_____

_____

_____

_____

_____

_____

_____

_____

_____

_____

_____

_____

Answer key
"Losers" who weren't

Answers will vary. Here is one example:

REAL losers are people who never even play the game or, if they do, they play only half-heartedly. They have no enthusiasm for anything, and they are disgusted with people who do. REAL losers not only drag themselves down but also bring down the spirits of everyone else around them. If they lose a game or an election, they make everyone around them miserable with their whining and complaining.

Sometimes so-called "winners" are actually losers. When people win an election by telling lies and making promises they cannot keep, they are just as much losers as those they defeated.

Eliot N.

Short for what?

When we hear the word "veteran," we often think of people who have served in the wars. Actually, a veteran is anyone who has served in a branch of the Armed Forces, whether during war or during peace time. The branches of the service are the Army, the Air Force, the Navy, the Marines and the Coast Guard.

Here is a list of terms and words that are associated with the Armed Forces. You may have heard many of them in movies, books or television shows. Now find out what they mean by doing "people research." In other words, talk to real people to find the answers. Perhaps one of your parents was in the service, or an uncle, a grandparent or a friend. Perhaps one of them was married to someone in the service. Perhaps some of your teachers served in the Armed Forces, or your neighbors, or the parents of friends. See how many of the items you can identify by talking to people.

1. WAC _____
2. MASH _____
3. GI _____
4. PFC _____
5. KP _____
6. Infantry _____
7. mess hall _____
8. fatigues _____
9. dog tags _____
10. M-16 _____
11. K rations _____
12. ROTC _____
13. Purple Heart _____
14. barracks _____
15. DMZ _____
16. VFW _____
17. AWOL _____
18. brig _____
19. howitzer _____
20. USS Enterprise _____
21. D-Day _____

22. OCS _____

23. blitzkrieg _____

24. admiral _____

25. POW _____

26. midshipman _____

27. tracers _____

28. Medal of Honor _____

29. friendly fire _____

30. civvies _____

31. taps _____

32. MIA _____

33. minesweeper _____

34. Kamikaze _____

35. agent orange _____

36. MP _____

37. Navy SEALS _____

38. leatherneck _____

39. draft board _____

40. ensign _____

41. U-boat _____

42. paratroopers _____

43. cavalry _____

44. top brass _____

45. *Stars and Stripes* _____

46. furlough _____

47. dog fight _____

48. B52 _____

49. West Point _____

50. stealth fighter _____

Answer key
Short for what?

1. WAC — Women's Army Corps
2. MASH — mobile army surgical hospital
3. GI — government issue
4. PFC — private first class
5. KP — kitchen patrol (kitchen duty)
6. Infantry — the branch of the Army that fights on the ground
7. mess hall — dining hall
8. fatigues — clothing worn by Armed Forces personnel for work or field duty
9. dog tags — metal identification tags worn by Armed Forces personnel
10. M-16 — a type of rifle
11. K rations — field rations (meals), now called MRE (Meals Ready to Eat)
12. ROTC — Reserve Officer Training Corps
13. Purple Heart — awarded to service personnel wounded in combat
14. barracks — a military dormitory
15. DMZ — demilitarized zone; a neutral area
16. VFW — Veterans of Foreign Wars
17. AWOL — absent without leave
18. brig — a navy jail
19. howitzer — a type of cannon
20. USS. Enterprise — an aircraft carrier
21. D-Day — June 6, 1944; the allied invasion of Normandy, France, in World War II
22. OCS — Officer Candidate School
23. blitzkrieg — swift, sudden military offensive used by Hitler in World War II
24. admiral — high-ranking officer in U.S. Navy and Coast Guard
25. POW — prisoner of war
26. midshipman — student at the U.S. Naval Academy
27. tracers — ammunition that lights up in flight to mark its path
28. Medal of Honor — highest U.S. military decoration
29. friendly fire — when troops get fired on accidentally by their own troops
30. civvies — what military personnel call their civilian clothes
31. taps — song played on bugle at the end of the day and at military funerals
32. MIA — missing in action
33. minesweeper — a ship used to destroy mines
34. Kamikaze — Japanese suicide pilots active during World War II
35. agent orange — chemical used to defoliate the jungle in Vietnam
36. MP — Military Police
37. Navy SEALS — elite group of Navy commandos
38. leatherneck — nickname for a Marine (Their collars used to be leather.)
39. draft board — a board that selects men for compulsory military service
40. ensign — low-ranking commissioned officer in U.S. Navy and Coast Guard
41. U-boat — German submarine used extensively in World War II
42. paratroopers — troops who jump out of airplanes
43. cavalry — troops who fight on horses or in armored vehicles
44. top brass — commanding officers
45. *Stars and Stripes* — a publication for military personnel overseas
46. furlough — leave of absence from duty
47. dog fight — two aircraft engaged in air-to-air combat
48. B52 — heavy bomber used in Vietnam and Iraq
49. West Point — site of United States Military Academy
50. stealth fighter — aircraft that avoids detection by radar

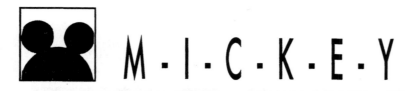

M·I·C·K·E·Y

November 18, 1928, was the birthday of Mickey Mouse, who may be the most famous animal in cartoon history. In honor of his birthday, take some time to think about other famous animals — animals from cartoons, comic books, movies and television. See if you can think of one or more famous animals that begin with each letter of the alphabet.

Give yourself one point for each animal you have correctly named. Subtract one point for each letter without any animal names. A score of 40 is excellent.

Animals   ## Scores

A _____   _____

B _____   _____

C _____   _____

D _____   _____

E _____   _____

F _____   _____

G _____   _____

H _____   _____

I _____   _____

J _____   _____

K _____   _____

L _____   _____

M _____   _____

N _____   _____

O _____   _____

P _____   _____

Q _____   _____

R _____   _____

S _____   _____

T _____   _____

U _____   _____

V _____   _____

W _____   _____

X _____   _____

Y _____   _____

Z _____   _____

Total score   _____

Answers will vary. Here are some possibilities:

Animals	Scores
Andre (the seal)	1
Barney, Bambi, Babe	3
Chip (of Chip and Dale)	1
Donald Duck, Dino	2
Eeyore	1
Felix the Cat, Flipper	2
Goofy, Garfield	2
Huckleberry Hound	1
Itchy (from "The Simpsons")	1
Jiminy Cricket	1
Krazy Kat	1
Lady (from Lady and the Tramp), Lassie	2
Mighty Mouse, Morris the Cat	2
Ninja Turtles	1
Odie	1
Porky Pig	1
Q	-1
Rocky	1
Snoopy, Sandy (from Annie)	2
Tigger, Tweety Bird, Toto	3
Underdog, Ugly Duckling	2
Velveteen Rabbit	1
Winnie the Pooh	1
X	-1
Yogi Bear	1
Z	1

Total: 33

Famous bills

November 23, 1859, was the birthday of the famous outlaw, Billy the Kid. Instead of honoring an outlaw, take a look at all the famous "bills" there are in history. See if you can think of a famous "bill" that fits each definition below. (Hint: Remember that "Bill" has many forms — William, Will, Willy, Billy, etc.)

1. Texan and once-presidential candidate Ross Perot is a

   ___ __ __ __ __ __ __ __ __ __ __ .

2. This rapper from Philadelphia is better known as a "prince" on TV and a hero on the big

   screen: __ __ __ __ __ __ __ __ __ .

3. Title of a "whale" of a movie: __ __ __ __ __ __ __ __ __ __

4. Hero who shot an arrow from 70 paces away through an apple placed on his son's head.

   __ __ __ __ __ __ __ __ __ __ __

5. Several of his plays have been turned into movies, including *Cat on a Hot Tin Roof.*

   __ __ __ __ __ __ __ __ __ __ __ __ __ __ __ __ .

6. In a folk song, singer begs him to come home:

   __ __ __ __ __ __ __ __ __ __ .

7. Nicknamed "Lady Day," she was known for such blues songs as "Strange Fruit" and

   "Driving Me Crazy": __ __ __ __ __ __ __ __ __ __ __ __ __ .

8. Player for the San Francisco Giants who was one of the few to achieve more than 3,000

   hits and 600 home runs in his career: __ __ __ __ __ __ __ __ __ __

9. Folksy humorist who is often quoted: __ __ __ __ __ __ __ __ __ __ __ .

10. What comes in the mail and makes adults grumble: __ __ __ __ __

11. This comedian wasn't really a doctor, but he played one on TV in his self-titled sitcom:

    __ __ __ __ __ __ __ __ __ __ .

12. Wild West Show performer named for killing nearly 5,000 buffalo in eight months:

    __ __ __ __ __ __ __ __ __ __ __ __ .

13. Fictional owner of chocolate factory __ __ __ __ __ __ __ __ __ __ __ __

14. New York football team: __ __ __ __ __ __ __ __ __ __ __ __ __ __ .

15. Tennis player who won 20 Wimbledon titles, 13 U.S. titles, four French titles and two

    Australian titles: __ __ __ __ __ __ __ __ __ __ __ __ __ .

16. Former "Saturday Night Live" comedian who starred in *Groundhog Day* and *Stripes*:

— — — — — — ⟨—⟩ — — —

17. First 10 amendments to the constitution:

— — — — — — — — — — —

18. Fairy tale animals tormented by a troll living under a bridge: — — — — —

— — — — — —   — — — — — —

19. Saxophone-playing president — — — — — — — — — — ⟨—⟩

20. This actor plays Starship Enterprise's Captain Kirk on "Star Trek":

— — — — — — — — — — — — — —.

21. This Pulitzer Prize poet of "This Is Just to Say" and "The Red Wheelbarrow" was also a

pediatrician. — — — — — — — —   — — — — ⟨—⟩ —

— — — — — — — — —

22. This is often read after someone dies: — — — —

23. The Academy Award-winning movie *Braveheart* was about this Scottish legend:

— — — — — — — — ⟨—⟩ — — — — —.

24. "Piano Man" known for other songs such as "Uptown Girl" and "Innocent Man":

— — — — — —   — — — —.

25. This cowboy legend's real name is James Butler Hickock.

— — — — —   — — — — — —   — — — ⟨—⟩ — — —

26. Actor behind TV's Incredible Hulk: — — — — —   — — — — — —.

27. The first Norman king of England: — — ⟨—⟩ — — — —

— — —   — — — — — — —.

28. This "City Slicker" also starred as Harry in *When Harry Met Sally*:

— — — — — — ⟨—⟩ — — —.

29. Song on Michael Jackson's *Thriller*: — — — — — —   — — — — —.

30. Unusually strange looking Australian mammal:

⟨—⟩ — — — — — — — — —   — — — — — — —

Match the circled letters in your answers to the numbers below.

"   ___ ___ ___ ___   ___ ___ ___ ___ ___   ___ ___   ___ ___ ___ ___ ___
   30 21 19 5   1   16 15 23 25   4   8   7   15 23 16 5

   ___ ___ ___ ___ ___ ___ ___ ___ ___ ___ ___ ___   ___ ___ ___ ___ ___ "
   4   8   23 28 7   8   1   16 15 23 25 8   7   15 23 16 5

        ___ ___ ___ ___ ___   ___ ___ ___   ___ ___ ___ ___ ___
        1   10 27 27 8   16 23 8   28 8   16 12 2

Answer key
Famous bills

1. BILLionaire
2. WILL Smith
3. *Free WILLY*
4. WILLIAM Tell
5. Tennessee WILLIAMs
6. BILL Bailey
7. BILLIE Holiday
8. WILLIE Mays
9. WILL Rogers
10. BILLs
11. BILL Cosby
12. Buffalo BILL
13. WILLY Wonka
14. Buffalo BILLs
15. BILLIE Jean King
16. BILL Murray
17. BILL of Rights
18. Three BILLY Goats Gruff
19. BILL Clinton
20. WILLIAM Shatner
21. WILLIAM Carlos WILLIAMs
22. WILL
23. WILLIAM Wallace
24. BILLY Joel
25. Wild BILL Hickock
26. BILL Bixby
27. WILLIAM the Conqueror
28. BILLY Crystal
29. BILLIE Jean
30. DuckBILLed Platypus

"Don't break my heart, my achy breaky heart."
BILLY Ray Cyrus

Thick as pea soup

The U.S.A. Dry Pea and Lentil Council sponsors National Split Pea Soup Week during the week of the second Monday of each November. You may or may not think split pea soup is worth celebrating, but you probably *have* heard someone say, "The fog was as thick as pea soup." If you have, you were hearing a *simile*.

A simile is a comparison that uses the words "like" or "as." In the example above, fog is being compared to pea soup. Another example: "The snowy hill was like a mound of mashed potatoes."

A *metaphor* is a comparison that does *not* use the words "like" or "as." A metaphor would be, "The snowy hill was a mound of mashed potatoes." Another example: "She was a bowl of warm Jell-O as she nervously waited to try out for the Olympics."

In honor of National Split Pea Soup Week, try writing some food metaphors and similes of your own. Below is a list of 60 types of food. Use these foods (or any others you can think of) to write 20 original similes and/or metaphors. Make them as descriptive and interesting as possible.

Example

food: grapefruit
simile: *Wayne was like a grapefruit; he was good for me, but I still didn't like him.*

apples
asparagus
bacon
bananas
Big Mac
blue cheese
bread pudding
broccoli
brussels sprouts
burrito
butter
carrot
cheeseburger
chicken chow mein
chicken fried steak
chicken gumbo
chocolate chip cookies
cooked spinach
crab legs
fat-free potato chips
fettucini alfredo
fish sticks

fried rice
grape popsicle
grapefruit
hoagie sandwich
hot fudge brownie
    sundae
ice cream sandwich
Jell-O fruit salad
jelly-filled donuts
lasagna
lemon meringue pie
liver
lobster tail
macaroni and cheese
marshmallows
milk shakes
peach pie
peanut butter and
    jelly sandwich
pepperoni pizza
pickled pigs' feet
pineapple

pork rinds
potato chips
radishes
red beans and rice
Reese's Peanut Butter
    Cups
Rice Krispies
root beer float
salad dressing
scrambled eggs
Snickers bar
spaghetti and meatballs
steak
sushi
Swiss cheese
taco
Thanksgiving turkey
tofu
tuna casserole
veggie burger
walnuts
zucchini

Answer key
Thick as pea soup

Answers will vary. Here are some examples:

1. The desert was as dry as liver.
2. My best friend and I are a peanut butter and jelly sandwich.
3. The gossip was as juicy as fresh pineapple.
4. Kate is all-American, like a cheeseburger on the 4th of July.
5. Monica's story was hard to swallow, like scrambled eggs without ketchup.
6. She felt as ordinary as macaroni and cheese out of a box.
7. Max is a lobster tail — a luxury I can't afford.
8. Jen was as tart as lemon meringue pie.
9. After working on the car, Alice was as greasy as pepperoni pizza.
10. That mechanic was as slimy as egg drop soup.
11. The picnic took a turn for the worse, like the Jell-O fruit salad that had been sitting out all day.
12. The turnout for the party was as huge as the four-foot submarine sandwich in the back room.
13. From swimming so much, Jill's once beautiful blonde hair was cooked spinach.
14. Paul was as tough as chicken fried steak at a truck stop.
15. The pickpocket had fingers like a melting grape popsicle in the middle of August.
16. Vivian was as rich as a hot fudge brownie sundae.
17. Kurt's version of the story had as many holes as Swiss cheese.
18. Hank wanted to go to the opera as about as much as he wanted to eat fat-free potato chips with no salt.
19. Gaby's whisper was as quiet as Rice Krispies that had been sitting too long in milk.
20. Our raft folded in the rapids like a big taco.

Top-notch tender turkey day

When we think of Thanksgiving Day we usually think of food — lots and lots of food. See if you can think of a food that begins with each of the letters in THANKSGIVING DAY. Then think of an adjective that begins with the same letter to describe each food.

Examples

Nervous noodles
Gross graham crackers

T _____

H _____

A _____

N _____

K _____

S _____

G _____

I _____

V _____

I _____

N _____

G _____

D _____

A _____

Y _____

Bonus

Use all your foods and their adjectives in a story about a Thanksgiving dinner. (Your story may have to be about a Thanksgiving that is not very traditional!)

Answer key
Top-notch tender turkey day

Answers will vary. Here are some possibilities:

Tantalizing turkey
Huge ham
Attractive apples
Nervous noodles
Kind kiwi
Scrumptious squash
Golden gravy
Incredible ice cream
Virtuous vegetables
Interesting iced tea
Nasty navy beans
Gross graham crackers

Delectable doughnuts
Artificial anchovies
Yummy yams

Bonus

I had to get used to the fact that this holiday was not going to be like the rest. It would just be my mom and me this year, and she had accepted an invitation to have Thanksgiving with a bunch of hippies living in a commune. They were old friends of hers from college, but I didn't know any of them.

When we got there I was surprised that there was any food at all. The place looked pretty run down. On the porch, I saw a basket of **attractive apples**, picked from the trees growing on the land. Inside on the kitchen table was a plateful of **delectable donuts**, straight from the frying pan and rolled in sugar. A **tantalizing turkey** and a **huge ham** roasted in the oven of a large wood-burning stove.

A pitcher on the counter was filled with a most **interesting iced tea**, bright red with slices of **kind kiwi** floating on top. I say "kind" because it looked too nice to eat. I was just thinking this might not be so bad when I saw the bowl of **nasty navy beans** on the counter. The pasta boiling in the black pot jiggled like **nervous noodles** — all wiggly and squirmy. Who has pasta and navy beans on Thanksgiving?

I went to explore the rest of the house and found a bedroom. A box with leftover pizza was stashed in the corner. When I peeked inside, I saw what had to be **artificial anchovies**. Nothing that dried up and ugly could be meant for human consumption. A small boy walked in. He was stuffing his mouth with really **gross graham crackers**.

When it was time for dinner, I slowly made my way back to the kitchen. I was relieved to see dishes of **yummy yams** and **scrumptious squash** being pulled out of the oven. My mom calls these foods "**virtuous vegetables**" because they are so good for you. A man stirred a pan of positively **golden gravy** on the stove. It looked so good my mouth started to water.

The meal was pretty good and the company was definitely interesting. But the biggest surprise was that dessert was not pumpkin pie but homemade ice cream, my favorite thing in the world. It was the most **incredible ice cream** I had ever eaten. This ending to the meal made the unusual Thanksgiving worth it all.

Blake P.

December

What money can't buy

December is Safe Toys and Gifts Month. It was created by Prevent Blindness America to educate people about choosing gifts that are safe for children.

One kind of gift that can't cause injuries is an intangible gift — a gift like "no nagging about wet towels on the floor" for a month, or "three nights of free baby-sitting" or "making your bed every day for a week."

In honor of Safe Toys and Gifts Month, list below 20 intangible gifts that *you* would like to receive. (When you are finished, you might considered giving some of the gifts to some-one else. If you would like them, chances are that someone else would, too.)

1. _____
2. _____
3. _____
4. _____
5. _____
6. _____
7. _____
8. _____
9. _____
10. _____
11. _____
12. _____
13. _____
14. _____
15. _____
16. _____
17. _____
18. _____
19. _____
20. _____

Answer key
What money can't buy

Answers will vary. Here are some possibilities:

1. Not having to do the dishes for a week
2. Not having to listen to Aunt Laura tell about her gall bladder operation again for at least two years
3. Not having to clean the litter box for a month
4. One whole day to slob around and be lazy
5. Permission to talk on the phone for as long as I want
6. An extra hour tacked onto my curfew one night
7. Having two friends stay overnight without my little brother driving us crazy
8. Being allowed to drink as many sodas as I want in one day
9. Talking to my boyfriend on the porch without any parental peeks from inside
10. Sleeping until noon on Saturday
11. Unlimited access to my sister's clothes for a month
12. A week of no history homework
13. A month of not having to empty the dishwasher
14. No comments from my parents about my haircut for a month
15. Being able to watch *The Sound of Music* again, with no complaints from my brother or my dad
16. Having no one call me "Shorty" for a year
17. No dog clean-up in the yard for a month
18. Having someone take me to school every day for a month, so I don't have to ride the bus
19. A whole day to do nothing but read a great book
20. Getting the shower first in the morning for a month

Sounds of a scene

On December 16, 1770, Ludwig van Beethoven was born. Although he began to lose his hearing at the height of his career, Beethoven continued composing until his death in 1827.

Celebrate Beethoven's birthday by exploring sounds. First brainstorm as many sounds as you can. See if you can add to the list below, to make 25.

1. faucet dripping
2. gum popping
3. shoe tapping
4. sprinkler sprinkling
5. car screeching
6. hammer pounding
7. _____
8. _____
9. _____
10. _____
11. _____
12. _____
13. _____

14. _____
15. _____
16. _____
17. _____
18. _____
19. _____
20. _____
21. _____
22. _____
23. _____
24. _____
25. _____

Choose four of the sounds and use them to describe a scene.

Example

Sounds:

shuffling feet
fingernails tapping
fire drill sounding
lawn mower humming

Scene:

How was I supposed to do well on my math test? Megan Olsen was sitting behind me and driving me crazy with the sound of the tapping of her three-inch purple fingernails on the desktop, over and over, over and over. Then, just as I was about to get the answer to the first story problem, the fire alarm sounded. We had been through fire drills a hundred times before, so we all loafed out the door. The air was filled with the sounds of shuffling feet and our complaining. I heard the lawn mower humming and looked over at Les, the school custodian. I felt jealous. Why couldn't I be like him, mowing the lawn in the sunshine and listening to music on my Walkman?

Answer key
Sounds of a scene

Answers will vary. Here are some possibilities:

1. ice cracking
2. wolf howling
3. cow mooing
4. pages turning
5. phone ringing
6. clock ticking
7. fingers tapping
8. knuckles popping
9. ball bouncing
10. laughter
11. key turning in a key hole
12. teeth chattering
13. door slamming
14. computer saving to a disk
15. egg cracking
16. someone chewing ice
17. clothes tumbling in a dryer
18. someone sweeping
19. iron steaming
20. door bell
21. printer printing
22. garbage truck
23. thunder
24. car honking
25. horse neighing

Choices: tapping fingers, pages turning, clock ticking, horse neighing

Scene:

As I sat on the green vinyl love seat in the waiting room, I heard the woman next to me nervously tapping her fingers on the table. I'd had a cold all week, so I was a little edgy. Just when I thought I couldn't take the tapping any longer, she picked up a magazine, and I heard the pages turning quickly. She must have just been looking at the pictures because nobody can read that fast. I was getting a little impatient as I listened to the big brown clock ticking away yet another minute. Suddenly I heard a neighing sound. The doctor burst through the doors, pulling the reins of the biggest horse I'd ever seen. The woman next to me jumped up. "Clyde! You're all right. I was so worried. Let's go home now and get you some nice warm chicken soup. How does that sound?" Clyde just sniffled a little as they walked out the door.

Todd T.

Nursery rhymes for a new century

Mother Goose is updating her nursery rhymes to appeal to children of the '90s. She's finally realized that today's kids don't really know what *curds and whey* are and that they would probably gag if they *did* know. Help out Ms. Goose by re-writing your favorite nursery rhyme.

Example

> *Little Bo Peep has lost her keys*
> *and can't drive to the ball game.*
> *She laced up her Nikes*
> *And then took a hike-y.*
> *And that's when it started to rain.*

If rhyming isn't your thing, write your version in paragraph form:

> *There was an old woman who lived in a shoe. Although it was a size eleven Reebok high-top, it was still too small to comfortably accommodate her extremely large family. After giving the kids some seven-grain fiber-enriched whole wheat bread, she gave them a severe talking to about their behavior and put them to bed. Then she called a real estate agent. He must have been a pretty good one because three weeks later the old woman and all her kids moved into a pair of very handsome spectator pumps with a roomy three-inch heel.*

Here's a list of other nursery rhymes that could use some re-vamping, but feel free to use other nursery rhymes instead:

Jack and Jill
Hey Diddle, Diddle!
Sing a Song of Sixpence
Mary, Mary, Quite Contrary
Little Miss Muffet
Little Boy Blue
Little Jack Horner
Jack Sprat
Jack Be Nimble
Pease Porridge Hot

Answer key
Nursery rhymes for a new century

Answers will vary. Here is one example:

Miss Shirley Muffet
sat on a park bench
eating her yogurt
that day.

Along came a mugger,
one meaning to slug her.
She maced him,
and he ran away.

> Riley F.

A cliché a day

"Look on the bright side" is an old saying that has become a cliché. A cliché is an expression that has been used so much that it doesn't have much originality. It has become dull from overuse.

For example, "quiet as a mouse" is a cliché. We have heard the phrase so often that we don't pay much attention to the words now. We never stop to think about mice and how they scurry around almost soundlessly. For most of us, a mouse never even enters our thoughts.

In honor of "Look on the Bright Side Day," see if you can give some old clichés a new twist. Below are just the beginnings of some familiar clichés. Make them fresh and new by writing new endings.

Example

Where there's a will, there's . . . .
a corpse.

1. The grass is always greener _____

2. Don't judge a book by its _____

3. Time heals _____

4. Every cloud has _____

5. A bird in the hand _____

6. A penny saved _____

7. You can lead a horse to water _____

8. A rolling stone _____

9. Cleanliness is next to _____

10. What you don't know _____

11. A stitch in time _____

12. You can't have your cake _____

13. Absence makes the heart _____

14. Ignorance is _____

15. A little learning _____

16. Don't cry over _____

17. Boys will be _____

18. Don't put all your eggs _____

Answers will vary. Here are some possibilities:

1. The grass is always greener when you water and fertilize properly.
2. Don't judge a book by its high price tag.
3. Time heals better than first aid cream and a Band-Aid.
4. Every cloud has a really long scientific name.
5. A bird in the hand could be messy.
6. A penny saved is pretty much worthless.
7. You can lead a horse to water, but don't expect him to do the backstroke.
8. A rolling stone is something to stay out from under.
9. Cleanliness is next to "clean cut" in the dictionary.
10. What you don't know you can look up in the reference section of your local library.
11. A stitch in time makes about as much sense as a hem in a black hole.
12. You can't have your cake if you are on a diet.
13. Absence makes the heart murmur words of love.
14. Ignorance is overrated.
15. A little learning is all your teacher asks of you.
16. Don't cry over a girl who dumped you.
17. Boys will be jerks sometimes.
18. Don't put all your eggs at the bottom of a grocery bag full of canned beans.

Whine, whine

Nobody likes a whiner. Whining is annoying, and it accomplishes nothing. Still, most of us at least *feel* like whining from time to time.

To celebrate National Whiner's Day, go ahead and whine about something. Here's your chance to whine without restraint, without guilt, and without your mom, dad, teacher or anyone else telling you to grow up. There is only one rule: You MUST whine about something unimportant.

Perhaps your shoe lace came untied and, when you walked by a mud puddle, the lace got soaked. When you finally got a break in your busy schedule to tie it up again, your fingers got a little dirty. Then, at dinner, that heartless woman you thought was your mother yelled at you for having dirty fingernails. If only that puddle hadn't placed itself right in your path! Poor you!

Whatever you decide to whine about, try to persuade your reader that this is one of *the* worst things that could possibly have happened to you. (When you share your story with the class, everyone should give a loud and sympathetic "Ohhhhh" after your sad tale.)

_____

_____

_____

_____

_____

_____

_____

_____

_____

_____

_____

_____

_____

_____

_____

_____

_____

_____

_____

Answer key
Whine, whine

Answers will vary. Here is one possibility:

I had just made a piece of toast with grape jelly. Then I tripped over the cat, and the toast flew out of my hands and landed on the new white carpet. The dog ran through it because he was chasing the cat. He got grape jelly all over his paws and tracked it all through the living room and up on the bed and onto my sheets because I hadn't had time to make my bed. That's because I was late getting up because I kept hitting the snooze button after staying up too late talking to Angelica about what to wear at the party at Jeff's house Saturday. It's all Jeff's fault for having a party!

Andie B.

Strike!

The bowling ball was invented December 29, 1862. Think about the words "bowling ball." They are usually understood to mean "a ball that is used for bowling." Taken more literally, however, the words can conjure up an image of a ball wearing ugly shoes and a polyester shirt, and getting a strike:

Look carefully at the pairs of words below and think about how you might look at them in a new way. Pick three different pairs of words and create illustrations for your new interpretations.

Creamed corn
Winding trail
Babbling brook
Shaved ice
Roaring river
Rolling pin
Rolling hills
Baking pan
Jumping jack
Whispering pines

Chattering teeth
Ironing board
Freezing rain
Snappy dresser
Waving flag
Hiking boots
Playing cards
Running water
Drinking glass
Operating table

Answer key
Strike!

Answers will vary. Here are some possibilities:

Running Water

FREEZING RAIN

WHISPERING PINES

Other books from Cottonwood Press

BEYOND *Roses Are Red, Violets Are Blue* —
  A practical guide for helping students write free verse $18.95

Dismissed!
  A cartoon notebook for teachers $7.95

Homework's Not Another Word for Something Else to Lose —
  Helping students WANT to succeed in school and then setting them up for success $19.95

Hot Fudge Monday —
  Tasty ways to teach parts of speech to students
  who have a hard time swallowing anything to do with grammar $18.95

Short and Sweet —
  Quick creative writing activities that encourage imagination, humor and enthusiasm for writing............$10.95

Journal Jumpstarts —
  Quick topics and tips for journal writing $7.95

Ideas that Really Work!
  Activities for English and language arts $21.95

Surviving Last Period on Fridays and Other Desperate Situations —
  Cottonwood game book $14.95

Games for English and Language Arts $16.95

Did You Really Fall into a Vat of Anchovies? —
  Games and activities for English and language arts $18.95

ImaginACTION —
  Using drama in the classroom, no matter what you teach $14.95

Writing Your Life —
  Autobiographical writing activities for young people $14.95

When They Think They Have Nothing to Write About . . .
  Cottonwood composition book $14.95

Hide Your Ex-Lax Under the Wheaties —
  Poems about schools, teachers, kids and education $7.95

If They're Laughing, They're Not Killing Each Other —
  Ideas for using humor effectively in the classroom, even if you're not funny yourself $12.95

Row, Row, Row Your Class —
  Using music as a springboard for writing, exploration and learning..$12.95

and more!

**Call for a free catalog of practical materials
for English and language arts, grades 5-12.**
1-800-864-4297

To Order More Copies of A Month of Fundays

Please send me _____ copies of *A Month of Fundays*. I am enclosing $23.95, plus $3.50 shipping per book. (Colorado residents add 72¢ sales tax, per book.) Total amount $_____.

Name _____

(School) _____

Address _____

City _____ State _____ Zip Code _____

Method of Payment:

□Payment enclosed □Visa □MasterCard □Purchase Order

Credit Card# _____Expiration Date _____

Signature _____

Send to:

Cottonwood Press, Inc.
305 West Magnolia, Suite 398
Fort Collins, CO 80521
1-800-864-4297

**Call for a free catalog of practical materials for
English and language arts teachers, grades 5-12.**